SIMPLE
GPS
NAVIGATION

SIMPLE

GPS

NAVIGATION

MIK CHINERY

fernhurst
BOOKS

First published in 1994 by Fernhurst Books, Duke's Path,
High Street, Arundel, West Sussex, BN18 9AJ, UK

Printed in Hong Kong through World Print Limited

British Library Cataloguing in Publication Data:
A catalogue record for this book is available from the British Library.

ISBN 1-898660-00-X

Acknowledgements
The publishers would like to thank the staff of Trimble
Navigation (Europe) Ltd for their help with the manuscript and for
the use of equipment and facilities for photography.
   The charts on pages 78 and 80 are Crown Copyright, reproduced
from Admiralty charts with the permission of Her Majesty's
Stationery Office.
   The charts on pages 73 and 74 are reproduced with the permis-
sion of Barnacle Marine Ltd, and the charts on pages 51, 53 and 77
with the permission of Imray, Laurie, Norie & Wilson Ltd.

Photographic credits
British Telecom: page 60.
Tim Davison: pages 64, 69.
Tim Hore: page 8 (T).
Motor Boat and Yachting magazine: pages 7, 23, 24, 28, 49.
Navstar/Brookes & Gatehouse Ltd: page 8 (B).
PPL: cover (yacht).
Scorpio Marine: page 21.
Tom Sheppard: page 56.
Trimble Navigation (Europe) Ltd: cover (GPS), pages 16, 59, 90.
John Woodward: pages 14, 15, 17, 18, 25, 27, 29, 30, 32, 33, 36, 39,
42, 43, 44, 45, 46, 52, 55, 60, 61, 81, 84, 85.

DTP by John Woodward
Artwork by Jenny Searle
Cover design by Simon Balley

Contents

1 Introduction

Electronic navigation is at last becoming accepted as a viable, reliable alternative to the traditional navigation methods that have been developed over many decades. This does not mean that your charts, parallel rules and pencils should be thrown away, but they are fast becoming the 'back-up' system rather than the other way round. The best navigators use a combination of both systems, cross-checking between them to ensure maximum accuracy.

One exception is the art of navigating fast motor cruisers on long passages. Conventional navigation and chartwork is quite impossible on a 35-foot boat cruising at a leisurely 40 knots. As the boat bounces over the waves even reading the compass can be difficult! To open a paper chart is folly since the slipstream will tear it apart in seconds, and any attempt to take a handbearing compass reading is pointless. Under these circumstances 95 per cent of the navigation must be pre-planned, and on passage the electronic navigator becomes the prime system. This is normal procedure for the pilot of a small aircraft, who has to submit a flight plan to the airfield authority before departure.

For many people the problem with electronic navigation is its potential unreliability, and you may worry about what will happen if the power fails. Obviously you will have to fall back on traditional techniques, but this is no problem if you follow a systematic approach to accurate position plotting.

You *must* record your position at regular intervals, both to keep a check on your progress and to give you something to work from if your electrical systems break down. The actual time interval and recording method depends on your speed. On a sailing boat with a steady chart table you could take a position fix from the GPS every half hour or so and mark it on the chart. On a fast boat this interval should be reduced to 15 minutes or even less, and as chartwork could be difficult you can simply write down the position – or better still the range and bearing to the next waypoint – and note the time. You can compare this list with your 'pre-plan' list and tick off the waypoints as you pass them. In the event of a total electronics failure you can refer back to your last fix and proceed on your way using traditional methods.

Many people now have hand-held GPS navigators, and some even buy them as back-up sets. As these units are battery powered you can save the day if your ship's power supply fails by switching on the back-up. For this to work, however, you must pre-plan your trip and enter the waypoint details in the back-up unit as well as the main set.

ELECTRONIC SYSTEMS

Radio navigation systems have been with us for many years. RDF (radio direction finding) is the oldest. This system is based on a receiver fitted with a directional antenna. Rotating the antenna towards an RDF beacon gives a null – a suppression of an audible signal – and a compass mounted on the antenna gives a bearing of the beacon thus located. If another station is then

▼ *Traditional methods of navigation are virtually impossible when you're bouncing over the waves in a fast boat.*

▲ Using RDF takes practice and is often far from accurate.

▼ Loran C, like Decca, can give good results in the right conditions, but interference can degrade its accuracy.

selected and the process repeated, the crossing point of the two bearing lines indicates the position of the receiver.

The accuracy of such RDF fixes varies enormously and they have to be treated with care if radio reception is poor. Compared to other systems RDF is inaccurate and not easy to use. The beacons transmit on low-frequency bands and are very susceptible to interference and subsequent inaccuracies. Yacht rigging and other metal structures can cause problems, and proximity to land and changing atmospheric conditions can also affect accuracy. Consequently the RDF system is now virtually dead.

Hyperbolic systems – Loran and Decca – were developed during the latter part of World War Two to help the allied invasion forces in Europe. Accurate landfalls at specific times were essential to the success of the military landings. Although crude by today's standards these early radio navigation systems gave the allied forces good results and the rest is history.

Both Loran C and Decca employ signals generated by groups of four land-based transmitting stations: a

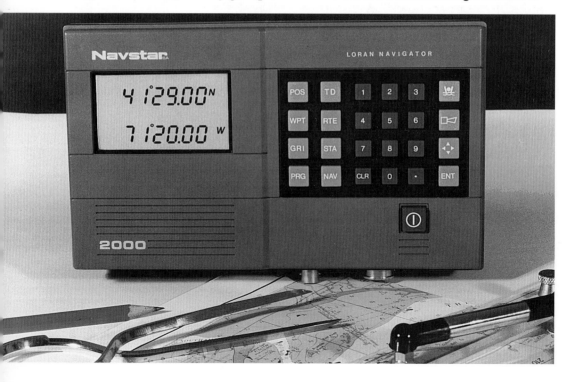

master and three slaves. The time or phase difference between the signals is measured within the receiver, and this gives a set of range figures; the receiver then uses these to calculate a position. Decca gives coverage extending up to 240 miles from the master station while Loran C coverage – although less accurate – extends approximately 1000 miles from the master station.

There are some fixed errors to be found on both these systems, and nightfall and sunrise/sunset times can cause skywave interference. However, during normal daylight hours in summer, in areas of good coverage, Decca can give repeatable positions to plus or minus 30 metres. Loran C is not so good, and plus or minus 300 metres can be considered a 'best' result.

On a winter night the situation deteriorates dramatically. Using Decca, the author has experienced errors of as much as eight miles on some occasions; Loran has been known to be 13 miles or more off-position. Nevertheless Loran C was widely adopted by the aircraft industry in the United States, especially in the private sector, and many chains of Loran C transmitters were built throughout the USA to provide a navigation system for small aeroplane users.

Along with Loran and Decca we also have Omega and Consul. In terms of accuracy Omega is not in the Decca/Loran class, but it is better than Consul. Like Decca and Loran C it is a hyperbolic system, but is designed to work over greater ranges and at lower RF frequencies. Corrections must be applied for the time of day, time of year and geographical location, yet even with all these variables taken into account its accuracy at sea level can still be several miles out.

Consul is a long range navigation system intended mainly for aircraft. Consul beacons transmit a pattern of dots and dashes which vary according to the sector you are in relative to the beacon. The pattern resembles the spokes of a wheel, with a different signal transmitted between each pair of spokes. By listening to the signal and counting the dots and dashes you can determine which sector you are in. Repeating the exercise with another one or two beacons gives a crossed bearing and an approximate position. Under favourable reception conditions this can give a fix accurate to within ten miles, but at night this figure can increase to 40 miles if you are 350-400 miles from a beacon.

All the radio navigation set-ups discussed so far use land-based transmitters based in different areas and different countries, and each station transmits signals which are picked up by special receivers unique to each service which calculate position information. They all have their uses but they all share one drawback. Because they operate on low radio frequencies they are susceptible to electrical interference and loss of signal quality. In Europe the strong Decca signals can degrade the Loran signals which are lie close alongside them on the waveband. Electrical interference from other on-board equipment can also cause havoc on the wavebands used by the receivers. Obviously when the signals are affected by any type of interference both the performance and accuracy of the systems suffer.

Transit

In order to overcome these deficiencies and give greater coverage and accuracy the American Department of Defense produced the first satellite navigation system during the early 1960s. The Navy Navigation Satellite System (NNSS), better known as Transit, was originally developed for the Polaris submarine missile programme, but in 1967 the system was released for private use and this paved the way for the production of dozens of dedicated Transit satellite receivers by many electronics manufacturers worldwide.

Transit consists of six satellites circling the earth in polar orbits at heights of between 600 and 1100 metres. Each continually transmits radio signals on two high frequency bands – 150 MHz and 400 MHz. Using these higher frequencies gives an immediate advantage as the sets are less susceptible to electrical interference and atmospheric conditions. The satellites pass overhead from horizon to horizon at irregular intervals depending on the orbits but normally 20 to 30 passes can be received in every 24-hour period.

The dedicated Transit receiver uses the doppler effect to work out a position from each satellite pass. In simple terms this can be equated with taking a running fix on each one as it travels overhead. Provided accurate inputs of the boat's speed and heading are given to the receiver the fixes can be accurate to within 200 metres or less, but because the doppler shift is a very accurate measurement of motion every knot of speed or drift error entered into the navigator can cause a fix error of 0.2 nautical miles.

The main disadvantage of this system is that fixes are computed only every hour or so, and sometimes two consecutive fixes may be separated by a gap of up to three hours. So although Transit is inherently more reliable and less interference-prone than Loran C or Decca, these hyperbolic systems are more accurate because they can give fixes that are updated every four minutes or less. Consequently the Transit system is seriously flawed, and it will cease to be funded by the USA by 1996. Presumably the satellites will die of old age, one by one. This may take some time, though; some of those in orbit are of 1967 vintage but they are still working well!

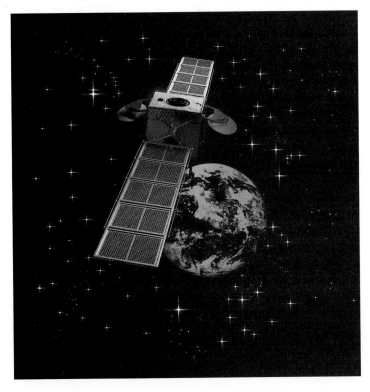

GPS – a new era

Any replacement for the Decca, Loran and Transit systems had to satisfy two main criteria:

1 The system had to employ satellites radiating high-frequency signals that could overcome radio interference, atmospheric aberrations and distortion caused by land masses.

2 The system had to provide continuous updating of position information.

These criteria have been met by GPS or, to give it its full title, the Global Positioning System. Like Transit, this is an essentially military system that has been funded by the government of the United States of America, but it is now available to anyone prepared to buy a receiver.

There are 21 GPS satellites, each orbiting the earth every 12 hours. These satellites are about 10,000 miles above the earth's surface and the orbits are inclined at 55 degrees to the equator. The spacing of the satellites is such that at least four are visible to a user anywhere in the world at any time. Each one transmits radio signals continuously on very high frequencies above 1200 MHz, and despite the very low power of the signals when they reach the earth they are virtually immune to most forms of electrical interference. And with at least four satellites in view at any one time even the slowest receiver can update its position every minute.

GPS works worldwide. It works at sea, in the middle of a desert, at the top of a mountain or in a rainforest clearing. As long as your receiver has a 'window' open to the sky you can find your position to within a few metres, night and day. Providing the set has at least three satellites in view it can compute an accurate two-dimensional fix (latitude and longitude) and this is all a boat skipper requires. If it has at least three satellites in view the set can compute a three-dimensional fix giving altitude as well as geographical position, and this is useful to hill walkers, mountaineers and pilots.

At present, and for the immediate future, the American DOD (Department of Defense) has reserved the right to 'scramble' the GPS signals. This is known as 'Selective Availability' or 'SA' for short. The outcome is that the positional accuracy is theoretically limited to plus or minus 100 metres for civilian use.

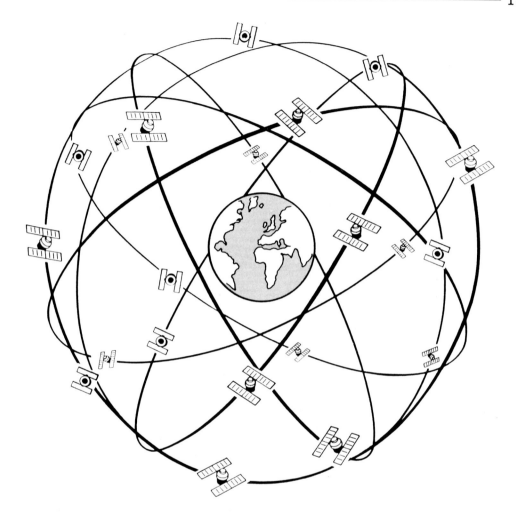

During the period of the Gulf War SA was switched off, and I then found the accuracy of GPS was plus or minus five metres! The long-term future of SA is unknown. Some experts say that it will remain switched on for some years while others say 'three years or so'. We will have to wait and see. In the author's experience the average fix error encountered when using GPS with SA is around 65 metres or less. Taking into account the consistency of the signal strengths and performance this is a small penalty to pay for safety and peace of mind.

▲ *The complexity of the GPS satellite con-stellation ensures that there are always at least three satellites in view at any time, from anywhere on earth.*

2 Choosing a set

Choosing a GPS set is rather like choosing a computer. First you are faced with a bewildering choice of manufacturers, some of which make at least six different models. Then you have to face an alien language of technical terms guaranteed to frighten away all but the most dedicated enthusiast. It's easy to lose track of exactly what you need, so let's try to determine what you require of your satellite navigation system.

First you have to consider the environment it is to be used in. Not many GPS units are fully waterproof: some are described as 'splashproof' or 'water resistant', but these terms should be treated with care. Completely weatherproofing any piece of electronic equipment is difficult and expensive, although you can buy sealed units that are internally gas-pressurised to keep the water out. If you anticipate that your GPS may receive harsh treatment from the elements, check carefully with the manufacturer that the unit is up to the job. 'Drowned' GPS navigators are not normally covered under the terms of the manufacturer's warranty.

▼ *If your GPS is to be mounted in an exposed position where it is likely to get wet you must make sure it is designed for the job.*

Once you have taken account of the working environment, you need to decide whether you want a portable, hand-held unit or a set that is built in to your boat, car or aeroplane.

Hand-held portables

A portable, self-contained set has some advantages. It is small and light enough to be carried in your pocket, and when you switch it on it will give you a position fix after a few minutes. You can be anywhere – at sea, in a desert or hiking in open country – and the GPS will tell you where you are.

There are a few disadvantages. The first is that the sets tend to eat batteries, so two or three hours' operation is all you can expect if you keep the set switched on all the time. Some units have a 'battery saver' mode in which the set effectively goes to sleep, switching on every few minutes to update itself. This mode can extend the battery life of the unit to two or three times the norm.

Another disadvantage is the physical size of the sets. They are miniaturised for portability, but this means that the displays are tiny and often difficult to read by those who do not have perfect eyesight. If you are bouncing over the waves on a high-speed boat it can be particularly difficult to focus your eyes on a small display.

Hand-held GPS navigators use an antenna mounted on the set. This means that the signals from the satellites can be screened or weakened unless you are out in the open. For example, if you are using the unit inside a boat wheelhouse, a car or an aircraft cockpit some loss of signal is inevitable. Some manufacturers have catered for this problem by including a socket for a separate, outside-mounted antenna.

Most sets can also be connected to a plug-in power lead to save the internal batteries. This enables the set to be mounted on a bracket and connected to a reliable antenna and power source, without sacrificing the option of unclipping it from its mounting and using it as a self-contained unit. This offers the best of both worlds – and also provides the added benefit of security against theft since you can remove the set at the end of the trip.

▼ *A lightweight hand-held GPS offers portability, but may not be appropriate for every application.*

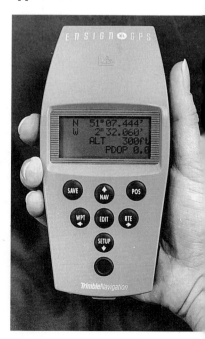

Fixed GPS sets

A fixed set is not self-contained and cannot be carried in your pocket. It has to be mounted in a dashboard or cockpit and wired to the main low-voltage power supply, and to get the best results you will need to fit an external antenna in clear air to give an unobstructed horizon-to-horizon view.

All this may sound inconvenient, but a larger, fixed set has plenty of advantages. The display is generally larger and easier to read, and because the set is built into a larger 'box' there is room for more memory chips which give an increased number of user facilities. Some of these extra facilities include the ability to connect (interface) the unit to other devices such as chart plotters, autopilots and instrument systems.

▼ *Most modern fixed units offer a host of features and large displays that are easy to read and interpret.*

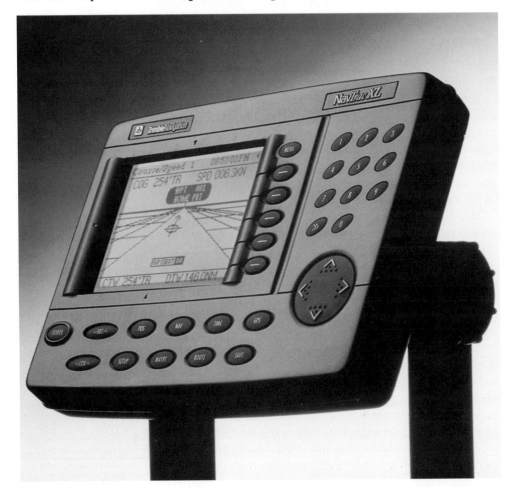

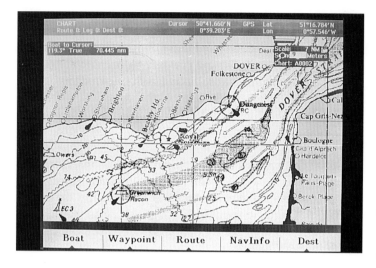

◀ A chart plotter displays charted information encoded on a disk or cartridge, and shows your track and position.

Most readers will be aware of chart plotters: electronic chart displays which use magnetic cartridges or CD-ROM disks loaded with digitised charts. There is also a type of plotter which simply shows your track, plus any waypoints, on a blank screen.

Plotters are available as separate units, but there are also several GPS/chart plotters on the market which have a GPS set and a plotter built into the same case. Taking the principle one step further, there are now sets that combine a GPS set, a plotter and an integral autopilot. Personally I am not too happy about such systems unless I have a back-up GPS in my pocket,

◀ The scale of the chart can be altered at the touch of a button to display more detail.

since if one part of the systems stops working then the other three may fail as well. On the plus side, however, a combined unit does have the advantage of reducing the 'box count' on your instrument panel, and it neatly avoids any problems associated with interfacing.

INTERFACING

Interfacing involves connecting electronic instruments by cables so they can listen and talk to each other. Units from the same manufacturer can usually be connected together without difficulty, but in the past there were often compatability problems between units from different manufacturers, owing to the wide variety of electronic 'languages' that were employed.

Thankfully a standard language has now been adopted by all electronics manufacturers to enable different items to be connected together without getting confused. This is known as the NMEA (National Marine Electronics Association) standard. The language has been updated several times to improve its usefulness, so the NMEA standard also carries a date. Currently the best one for your GPS is NMEA 0183, and almost every set on the market conforms to this specification.

▶ *A track plotter shows your position, track, waypoints and, in some models, other features such as navigation hazards. This type of plotter is ideal for users who need to know exactly where they have been, such as divers searching for a wreck site.*

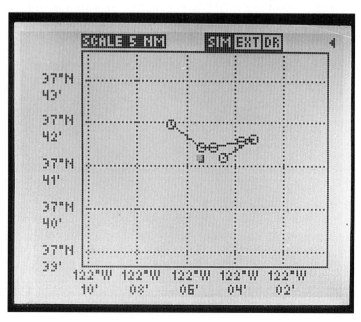

Interfacing enables information to be shared or compared to give a more accurate picture of the current situation; it also permits one unit to instruct another directly, without any input from the user. For example, on an interfaced system a GPS can compute an accurate speed-over-ground figure. It can then take the reading from the ship's speed log or the aircraft air speed indicator and compare the 'true' with the 'indicated' figure. This difference is the vector speed of the current or wind.

The GPS can also download your position into an electronic chart plotter. The computer-type display can then plot a dotted line on the screen showing your course and position. You can even interface your GPS to an autopilot so that it steers you directly towards a waypoint while automatically compensating for cross-currents and winds.

Modern radar sets are also 'NMEA compatible', which means that they will accept NMEA data from a GPS unit and display waypoint information on the screen. For example, if your next waypoint is 6.7 miles away the radar will show a circle on the display 6.7 miles away. If you are on course then the circle will be exactly ahead of your track. A dotted line points the way from the centre of the display to the circle, and together the dotted line and the waypoint circle look rather like a lollipop on a stick.

Using your GPS in this way is very simple, and I find that 'lollipop navigation' is really useful at night, particularly in close proximity to hazards. If you are negotiating a difficult river or harbour entrance it is reassuring to see your next waypoint showing between the harbour entrance piers on the radar display. This method of navigation is very new but it gives a good visual indication of your course-keeping.

TYPE OF RECEIVER

There are two basic types of GPS receivers. The less sophisticated type operates on a single channel and 'sequences' between satellites. This means that it listens to one and take some readings, then switches to the next one and so on. This switching is carried out very fast, enabling the readings to be computed together to give a position.

The more refined (and expensive) sets are multi-channel, and are able to track four or more satellites simultaneously. These units can be taking readings on one channel while the other is acquiring the next satellite. The performance of such a unit will usually be superior to that of a single-channel GPS, but to some extent the difference is academic. Any channel switching and subsequent computation takes place in seconds, so you receive fix updates every minute or so from the most basic of receivers.

Differential GPS

The most expensive GPS receivers are the 'differential' sets. Such a set works on the same principle – receiving signals from the satellites and processing the information to give a position – but potentially it offers greatly increased accuracy because it contains an additional receiver tuned into fixed, land-based GPS stations. Since the land-based stations are in known positions, any fixing error caused by the scrambled SA transmissions can be precisely quantified and broadcast to nearby differential GPS receivers. The receivers can then use this figure to correct the fixes that they are obtaining. Using this system you can expect fixes to be accurate to within a few metres –

▼ *A differential GPS station measures the offset between its known position and the 'scrambled' position information broadcast by the satellites, and transmits the correction to all differential GPS receivers in the vicinity.*

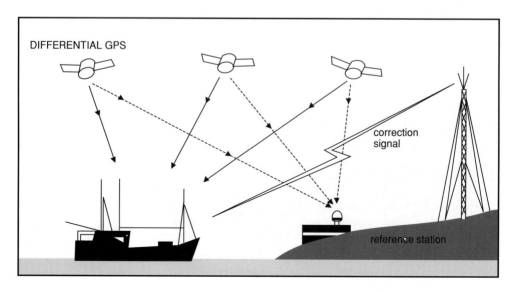

DIFFERENTIAL GPS

correction signal

reference station

indeed plus or minus five metres is probably the maximum error.

This sounds fine in theory but there are some disadvantages in practice. The differential GPS land stations do not provide comprehensive coverage, and tend to be restricted to important areas such as major ports and other heavy traffic zones. Secondly the integrated sets are considerably more expensive; alternatively you will need to buy an add-on box to connect to your existing receiver. The other problem is that not every country has differential GPS transmitters and some, like the UK, make an annual charge for the service which is more than the cost of the GPS set itself!

◀ A differential GPS ground station, close to a more familiar navigation aid.

3 ..... Installation

To get the best out of your GPS navigator you should mount it where it can be viewed comfortably by the helmsman or pilot. On boats, particularly, this may cause problems.

You may want to mount it in the cockpit – but is the set waterproof? If not, is there a waterproof repeater instrument available which would allow the main set to be mounted in a weatherproof position while the repeater is used outside?

If the set is to be mounted in an open position, can you read the display in bright sunlight? Many GPS receivers use liquid crystal displays (LCDs) and it is important to check the viewing angle to ensure the contrast is adequate in available light. Some sets can be viewed from only a limited angle of vision so the mounting angle can be critical. If the contrast can be adjusted this may help.

Once you have decided where to mount the device you will need to provide a power supply. Most sets will work on a DC voltage of between 10 and 40 volts, but please check the manual before you start wiring. If your boat or aircraft has a 24-volt system and the GPS is designed for 12-volt operation you will need to buy a voltage regulator.

If possible do not connect the set to the battery that is used for starting the engine. You could get a severe voltage drop when the engine is started, and this may cause the set to shut off as it detects low voltage on the power supply.

It is important to select the optimum antenna mounting point to ensure good reception from the satellites. Ideally the antenna needs a clear view from horizon to horizon in all directions. On a yacht the obvious place is the masthead, but this is not ideal as it is prone to large and rapid movements in rough seas. In fact the most practical antenna site on a yacht is usually the pushpit. On a motor boat the best site is usually on the radar arch, raised above the radar on a small stub mast. If you don't have a radar arch, consider mounting it above the metal windscreen surround.

You should keep the antenna away from VHF transmitter aerials and any large metal structures which
could screen it, and NEVER mount the antenna pod in
line with the output from a radar scanner. Most GPS
receivers have circuit boards and components inside
the antenna units, and strong radar transmissions
beaming directly into the antenna can cause irrepara-
ble damage to some internal components. Finally
beware of mounting the antenna in a position where
crew members can grab it to keep their balance;
unfortunately GPS antennas tend to be short and fat,
and just right for a handhold.

◄ *If you want access
to GPS information
from an exposed posi-
tion, such as the fly-
bridge of a fast
cruiser, consider
mounting the main
instrument safe below
and linking it to a
waterproof repeater.*

▲ *If you mount the antenna on or near the radar arch make sure it is well clear of the radar scanner itself – or the powerful radar signal will blow up your GPS. On this boat the GPS antenna is mounted on its own stub mast.*

When installing the antenna try to keep the downlead well away from other electrical cable runs, since this will cause interference and degrade performance. If your antenna is supplied with a long downlead ask the manufacturer whether it is permissible to cut and shorten it if your cable run is short. Sometimes the lead length is critical for the correct operation of the set. To confuse matters further, such are the standards of microelectronics these days that many manufacturers have built the entire GPS receiver into the antenna pod. In this case the downlead just connects the set with the display control panel and power supply. If your set is one of this type you must be extra careful to route the downlead out of harm's way. Some of these leads have up to 40 thin wires inside and will not put up with much physical abuse.

Once you have the power supply and antenna connected, all that is left to connect is the interface wiring.

◄ *On a yacht the pushpit is usually the best site for the antenna. The masthead is subject to too much random movement.*

The NMEA connections consist of a 'signal' lead and a 'ground' lead. Follow the instructions given by the manufacturer of the equipment you are connecting to your GPS navigator. Some autopilots, for example, have two NMEA inputs. This will allow both a GPS and a Decca or Loran C set to be connected, giving you a choice of which system you wish to drive the autopilot.

Most sets can send out NMEA signals in different formats, so consult your manual to see what your set is capable of putting out. As mentioned the most common and up-to-date is NMEA 0183, but your set will probably be able to send signals in other formats such as NMEA 0182 or NMEA 0180. Make sure you select the correct one for your autopilot or chart plotter. Provided each part of the interfaced system can talk and listen in the same language there will be no problems, but if you muddle them up then nothing will work correctly.

4 Initial programming

When you press the ON or PWR button to power up your GPS set the display will indicate the software version, and if it is a plotter GPS it will show a disclaimer notice; you will have to press the ENTER key to acknowledge this. Switching off is similar, except that you have to hold the ON or PWR key down for several seconds. During this period many sets display the message 'Turning off OK?' to check that you really intend to switch off.

When it is fresh out of the box your GPS receiver will need some essential information to help it lock onto the next satellite as it passes overhead. Initially the GPS receiver forms an 'almanac' – a calender of satellite passes – so it knows which one is coming next and the time of each pass. To help the set to get started you will have to key in the date and the correct time; either UTC (Universal Time Coordinate) or in some cases GMT. Ideally this should be entered as accurately as possible, but in practice plus or minus ten minutes is good enough. By the time the set has calculated the coordinates from the first satellite this time will have been corrected by the four super-accurate atomic clocks working in each of the GPS satellites.

The set will also ask you to enter your local time. You could just key in the time on your watch, but a better option would be an offset from the UTC time. For example, if your local time is five hours ahead of UTC (or GMT) you input the local time as plus five (+5). Your ETA (Estimated Time of Arrival) will then be displayed in your local time, rather than UTC or GMT.

If you are on a boat, the next thing to enter is the height of the antenna above sea level. Although this is not critical it can improve fix accuracy when the set is working with reduced satellite coverage and limited to 2D (two dimensional) fixes.

With some sets you can speed up the initial acquisition of satellites and the formation of the almanac by entering your approximate position on the earth. A latitude and longitude figure to within a couple of miles will speed things up.

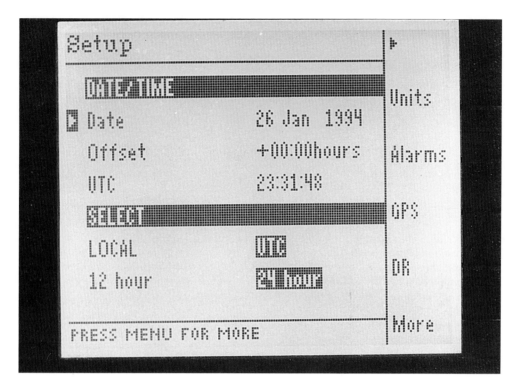

Setup   ▶

DATE/TIME   Units

▣ Date   26 Jan 1994

   Offset   +00:00hours   Alarms

   UTC   23:31:48

SELECT   GPS

   LOCAL   **UTC**

   12 hour   **24 hour**   DR

PRESS MENU FOR MORE   More

After the two most essential facts have been entered – the date and time – your navigator will start to work. Even the slowest models will 'find' themselves within 15 minutes. After this the almanac information is retained in the set's memory even if it is switched off for a few hours, and the next time it is switched on the acquisition time should be no longer than a couple of minutes.

▲ A time setup display. The date and time have been entered, and 24-hour time selected. Since in this case the local time is the same as the Universal Time Coordinate there is no time offset.

Magnetic variation

Unless you have entered a correction factor any bearings displayed will be in degrees TRUE – in other words, the bearings indicated on the chart rather than the bearings indicated by a compass. However, all sets have provision for magnetic variation correction.

Some have a facility called 'Auto mag' or 'Auto variation'. For this you just select AUTO (yes/no) and the unit will work out the magnetic variation for your area on the correct date. Wherever you go, the set automatically re-calculates the variation and displays the correct figure for your area.

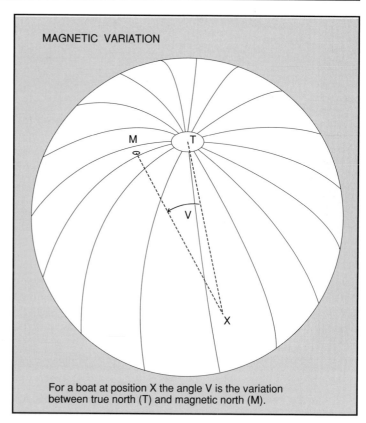

MAGNETIC VARIATION

For a boat at position X the angle V is the variation between true north (T) and magnetic north (M).

▶ *The position of magnetic north changes from year to year, and its effect on the compass varies according to where you are on the globe. The local offset, or variation, is given on the local chart or map, but many GPS sets will make the required correction automatically.*

If the set does not offer the Auto variation facility you will need to take some care. You can enter the current variation for your area, taken from the map or chart, and this will be correct as long as you are navigating within this area.

The snag is that this correction is applied *no matter where you are.* If you move a hundred miles or so the magnetic variation may be substantially different, but your GPS will be giving figures corrected for your start position.

For example, sailing south from Bermuda to Puerto Rico involves a trip of around 900 miles, and during the voyage the magnetic variation can change by up to 18 degrees. If you have entered a manual correction for variation at the beginning of the trip it will be seriously adrift as you approach a landfall at Puerto Rico. So if you think you may be undertaking long trips you would be well advised to choose a GPS set that has an Auto variation function.

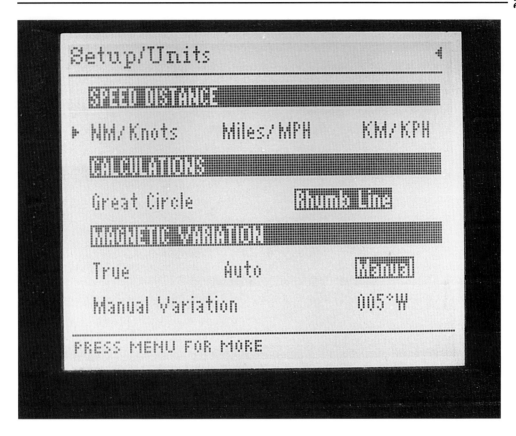

Setup/Units

SPEED DISTANCE

► NM/Knots   Miles/MPH   KM/KPH

CALCULATIONS

Great Circle   Rhumb Line

MAGNETIC VARIATION

True   Auto   Manual

Manual Variation   005°W

PRESS MENU FOR MORE

Deviation

Many units on the market have an entry page for magnetic deviation. This means that you can enter the corrections shown on your compass deviation card. After
this any bearings displayed will be related exclusively
to the ship's steering compass, so if you took a bearing
of a distant waypoint with a handbearing compass the
figure would differ from the one displayed on the GPS.
In the author's opinion this is a feature that should be
ignored. The possible confusions and errors that could
arise are legion. Just leave the setting at zero and forget it!

Units of measurement

There are many uses for GPS navigator sets in many
different places, and the displayed units of distance
and speed can be altered on most sets to suit the local
or professional conventions. People flying or boating
will need nautical miles and knots. Hill walkers,

*▲ Here the setup dis-
play is showing the
units of measurement,
the route type and the
magnetic variation.
The units are still to
be chosen, but the
operator has selected
a rhumb line route
and a manually-
entered variation of
five degrees west.*

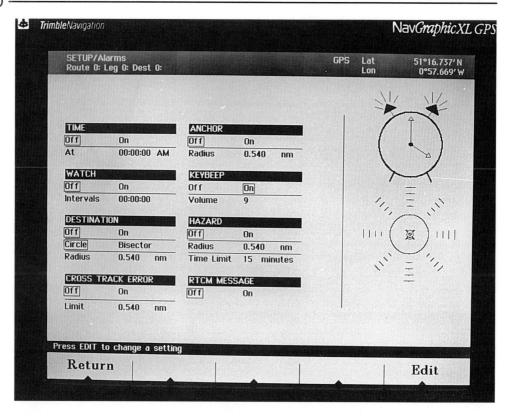

⚓ *TrimbleNavigation*   Nav*GraphicXL GPS*

SETUP/Alarms
Route 0: Leg 0: Dest 0:

GPS   Lat   51°16.737' N
      Lon   0°57.669' W

TIME			ANCHOR		
Off	On		Off	On	
At	00:00:00 AM		Radius	0.540	nm

WATCH			KEYBEEP		
Off	On		Off	On	
Intervals	00:00:00		Volume	9	

DESTINATION			HAZARD		
Off	On		Off	On	
Circle	Bisector		Radius	0.540	nm
Radius	0.540	nm	Time Limit	15	minutes

CROSS TRACK ERROR			RTCM MESSAGE		
Off	On		Off	On	
Limit	0.540	nm			

Press EDIT to change a setting

Return   Edit

▲ *This setup screen enables a variety of alarms to be activated, and also permits the various modes and limits to be defined.*

Antarctic explorers, desert crossers and participants in the Paris-Dakar Rally will need kilometres or statute miles. Luckily any of these three unit scales can be chosen according to your requirements.

Alarms

There can be dozens of reasons why a set will 'bleep' at you. Depending on the model, alarms can be set for everything from low battery voltage or a poor GPS fix to 'Arrived at waypoint'. What you choose to 'bleep' is your choice, since each alarm can be turned on or off at will.

The best approach is to go through the options one by one, instruction book in hand, and decide which are suitable for you. I personally use the following alarms: low battery voltage, waypoint approach, poor GPS fix and off-course cross-track alarm. I also occasionally set the alarm clock to give a regular 'bleep' to remind those on watch to enter the current position on the chart.

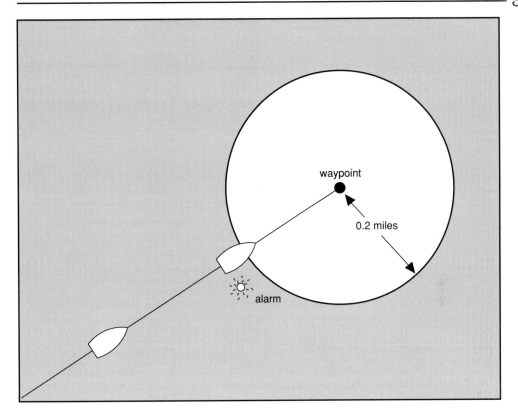

Memory

After you have entered all this initial information the receiver will start looking for and acquiring satellites as they appear. A new set can take as long as 15 minutes to initialise and form the almanac, but once the set is in commission it should only take a minute or two to initialise and come up with a fix.

All the programming information, including all entered waypoints and positions, is retained in the set's memory, and if the main batteries expire and you replace them the information is still retained. Every GPS navigator has a tiny lithium battery inside it which is charged while the set is in use. The charge will last for six months or more if the set is unused. These batteries do not last forever, though; about five years is the average life. If your navigator is a bit elderly and does not retain information after switch-off then the lithium battery is faulty and should be replaced. This is not a job for the user, so you will have to return the set to the dealer or manufacturer.

▲ *The waypoint alarm sounds at a user-defined distance from the waypoint, keeping you informed and switching the GPS to the next waypoint on the route plan. If the GPS is interfaced with an autopilot the boat will automatically change course towards the next mark.*

5 · Simple outputs

Most of the basic information a navigator needs can be displayed on your GPS at the touch of a button.

Position

The simplest output from the set is your position given in latitude or longitude or, if your set has the ability, in National Grid reference numbers. The position shown is updated every minute or less, even on receivers with the lowest specification, but for many forms of navigation a fix every 15 minutes or so is adequate.

When hill walking or climbing, for example, you will need to conserve battery life and since your over-the-ground speed is very low you will not have moved very far between fixes. In such circumstances a position update every half-hour or so could well be sufficient. On a yacht crossing the Pacific an accurate position every 12 hours is adequate until you come closer to land.

On a fast boat or aircraft the requirements are obviously different. For a start the set can be wired into the main low voltage supply so battery life is no problem,

▶ *The fundamental job of the GPS is to tell you where you are. Here the position is displayed as a set of lat-long coordinates for plotting on a chart or map, but most sets can show position information in a variety of ways.*

and if you are travelling fast or you are near obstructions then instant, frequent position updates are vital.

Whatever you use your GPS for, it is essential to
make a note of your position at regular intervals
depending on your ground speed. As previously mentioned it is not always possible to mark this on a map
or chart, but simply noting the lat/long figure and time
in a notebook will suffice. This way you have a constant
record of your progress to refer back to if you get
problems.

Speed and course

The speed and course are displayed in various ways
depending on the make of set you have. So you may
see figures for SMG, GS and SOG; these stand for
Speed Made Good, Ground Speed and Speed Over
Ground. If you see the abbreviations VTD, VTW and
WAS these stand for Velocity To Destination, Velocity
To Waypoint and Waypoint Approach Speed.

The first group are all showing your true speed over
the ground. You may be travelling faster through the
air or water, but wind and currents may be working
against you. The displayed figure takes any variables
into account, so it indicates the true speed you are
achieving.

▼ *This display is
showing a lat-long
position, plus the
course over ground,
the speed over
ground and the cross-
track error.*

| NAV/Text/Lat-Lon | | GPS | Lat | 51°16.674′ N |
| Route 0: Leg 1: Dest 450: SAVE | | | Lon | 0°57.699′ W |

Latitude	51°16.674' N	GPS	51°16.674′ N 0°57.698′ W
Longitude	0°57.698' W	DR	51°16.674′ N 0°57.698′ W
Course Over Ground	031.7° Mag		
Speed Over Ground	0.8 Knots		
Cross Track Error	0.003 nm Right		

▼ *VMG is important when you're sailing into the wind. Here boat A is beating at the optimum angle: the component of her speed towards her goal is X, which is her VMG. Boat B is pinching and sailing slowly, so her VMG is Y; boat C is sailing fast in the wrong direction, so her VMG is only Z.*

The second group is not so straightforward. If you are sailing towards a destination or waypoint the wind may be blowing from ahead of you, forcing you to tack back and forth. During these tacks you may well be moving through the water or over the ground at ten knots – but you are not aiming directly for your waypoint. In all probability you will be heading at 45 degrees to the bearing of the waypoint, so you are gradually getting nearer but you are not approaching at the speed you are travelling through the water. So your SMG (Speed Made Good) could be 10 knots, but your VTD (Velocity To Destination) may be only about seven knots or so.

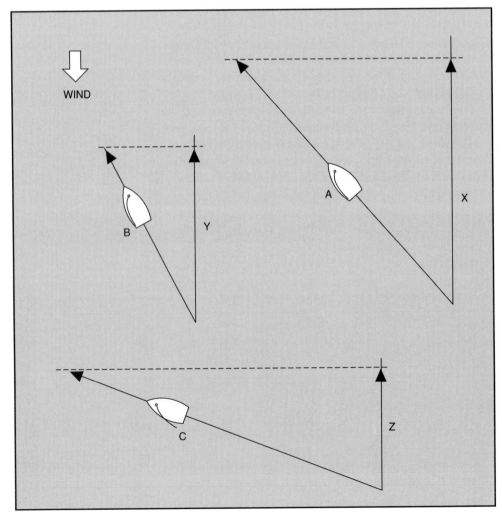

Course Made Good (CMG), Course Over Ground (COG) and Track (TRK) work in a similar way. This is the *actual* course you are achieving over the earth's surface or the seabed. You may well be steering 175 degrees, but if a crosswind or cross-current is pushing you off track your real course may be very different. The COG or CMG displayed takes this into account and gives the direction in which you are travelling over the ground.

Remember that unless you have entered the variation or selected auto variation the display will show degrees *true*. If either of the two former options have been selected then the display will show degrees

▼ *The course-over-ground (COG) display shows by how many degrees the boat is being pushed off-track by the tide (left). By applying the same figure as a correction to the course to steer, you can direct the boat straight down the track to the waypoint.*

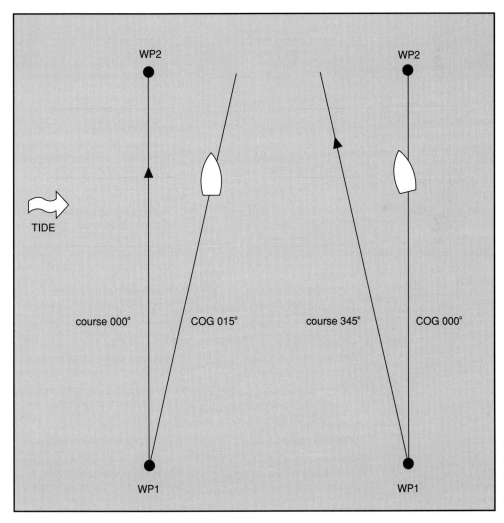

| NAV/Text/CD–DD | GPS | Lat | 51°16.748'N |
| Route 1: Leg 1: Dest 2: | | Lon | 0°57.582'W |

Course to Destination	**358.5°** Mag	COG	030.8° Mag
		SOG	3.2 Knots
Distance to Destination	**58.315** nm	Set	000.0° Mag
		Drift	0.0 Knots
Distance Made Good	**0.084** nm	Spd	0.0 Knots
		Hdg	000.0° Mag
Velocity Made Good	**2.7** Knots	XTE	0.056 nm
			Right
Estimated Time Of Arrival	**09:59+01** AM		
Time to Go	**21:43:51**		

Press a softkey to view a different Text screen

▲ *The course and distance to the next waypoint not only tell you which way to steer – they also offer a simple means of plotting your position on the chart. This display also shows the speed over the ground, the actual distance covered since the last waypoint, and the ETA.*

magnetic. In this case a small letter 'm' or 'c' is shown after the bearing. This stands for 'magnetic' or 'corrected'.

Accurate speed and course figures are essential navigation information. If you know your true speed and course you can check them against the compass and the boat's log or aircraft's airspeed indicator to quantify the effect that the winds and currents are having on your craft.

Range

Range, or the distance to the next waypoint, can be displayed as RNG, DTG or DIS. These terms stand for Range, Distance To Go and Distance. The figure may be expressed in sea miles, statute miles or kilometres, depending on how you set up your initial programming.

The distance can be shown as rhumb line or, for long passages, a calculated great circle route. You should normally select the rhumb line display, but if you are going transatlantic or transpacific then read on.

The earth is basically a sphere, so an arc of a great circle – a radius from the centre of the earth – will be the shortest distance between two points. On a great

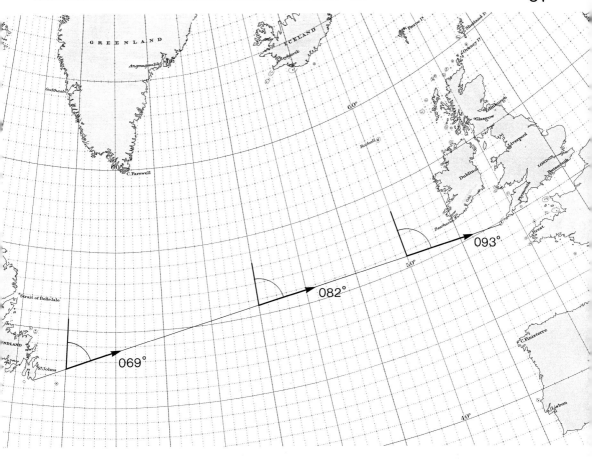

circle chart such an arc appears as a straight line, but the lines of longitude are not parallel; as you follow the 'straight line', therefore, its bearing relative to the longitude grid keeps changing. In other words, you would have to keep altering your compass heading to stick to the great circle track which, as we have seen, is the shortest route.

In practice the difference is negligible for distances of less than 600 miles, and for such trips it is best to avoid the complications of great circle route-planning and use rhumb line courses and distances. For greater distances, though, the savings can be significant. For example, the rhumb line course between Plymouth and Miami is 3840 nautical miles, while the great circle course is about 135 miles shorter at 3705 miles. Likewise the rhumb line course from Fremantle to Capetown is 4923 miles while the great circle course is

▲ *A great circle track appears as a straight line on a gnomonic (great circle) chart, but since the lines of longitude are not parallel the compass heading of the track is changing all the time. Happily the GPS will give you the right course to steer throughout the trip if you select the great circle option.*

4685 miles. If the course is more north-south oriented the differences are less, because a north-south rhumb line course *is* a great circle. Brisbane to San Francisco is 6188 miles by rhumb line, but the great circle route is only 41 miles less at 6147 miles.

Man overboard and quicksave

All GPS sets have some form of 'man overboard' or 'waypoint dump' function. This is usually activated by pressing a single button which immediately saves the present position in the machine's memory. The display then changes to show the distance and bearing back to that position (obviously the distance starts at zero and increases as you pull away). On some sets the lat/long position of the MOB is shown, and on others the position is automatically allocated a waypoint number. By calling up the waypoint number shown you can record the lat/long position.

It is vital to realise that the MOB position indicated is not necessarily the position of the casualty. Some time may have elapsed between the actual incident and the pressing of the button, and if there is any tide running the casualty will be swept downstream from the point where he fell off the boat. If the tide is running at four knots, the victim will be 135 yards away from the position indicated after only one minute! It is therefore essential to have a record of the time when the button was pressed. The display should show this, but the time can be taken from a wristwatch if necessary. This will give you – and the rescue services – something to work from.

Probably the best way to use the man overboard function is to return to the initial MOB position as quickly as possible and then head in the same direction as the tidal stream. Some sets offer you the option of entering the tidal set and rate; the unit will then compute a continuously updated position for the casualty, enabling you to return directly to his *calculated* position. Note that the GPS needs the correct tidal figures keyed into its computer before it can make this calculation, so make sure you have an up-to-date chart or tidal stream atlas aboard.

Losing someone overboard is every sailor's nightmare, and hopefully it will never happen to you. You

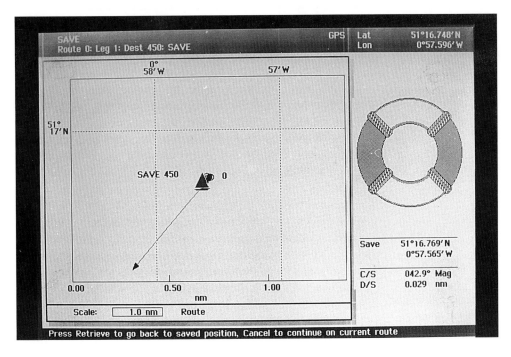

can still make use of the MOB button, though, because its basic function is to memorise, instantly, any position for future use. On some sets the function is more or less duplicated by a 'quicksave' button. For example, if you find a good fishing spot, you can press the button to memorise its position for future use. Or if you enter a difficult channel which you may need to use at night or in poor visibility you can record each change of course as a waypoint. On your return trip you simply navigate from point to point in reverse order.

Some top-of-the-range GPS units have a waypoint library and management facility which allows you to move waypoints around. For example, you may have entered some favourite places as Waypoints 3, 4 and 5, or you may have used a 'quicksave' function to memorise the points along a route. Later you may want to move them to a different location such as 51, 52 and 53. The management facility allows you to do this by copying from one location to another. So you can specify Waypoint 3 to be transferred to waypoint position 53 and so on. This saves re-keying waypoints into different memory positions, which is both time-consuming and vulnerable to keying errors.

▲ *The man overboard function memorises your position at the touch of a button, and switches the display to show a continuous update of the boat's position in relation to the original position of the MOB. It will also give you a course and distance to steer to return to the memorised position, and some sets will depict the situation on a track plotter.*

6 .... **Waypoint navigation**

A waypoint is simply a point you wish to sail or fly to. It can be a buoy, a harbour entrance, an anchorage, a point off a lighthouse, an airfield or a course-change point. Whatever it is, you need to know its position in degrees of latitude and longitude so it can be entered into the machine.

GPS is *very* accurate so take care when entering waypoint positions from a chart. For example, it is not prudent to enter the position of a lighthouse exactly, since in poor visibility you could actually hit it! Similarly you must be careful with buoys, since some of them are huge iron monsters which could wreck your craft. Enter the positions that *you* want to be in, not the positions of nearby reference points.

When you are making your passage plan remember that your GPS assumes your start position is Waypoint zero. The machine will give you a bearing and distance from this zero position directly to your first waypoint – and this could be through an area of shallows,

▼ *A conspicuous navigation mark such as this LANBY makes a tempting waypoint, but be sure not to enter its precise position. You could easily hit it!*

TAKING WAYPOINT POSITIONS OFF THE CHART

All charts have a border that shows latitude down the side and longitude across the top. By spanning the distance between your proposed waypoint and the nearest grid lines on the chart using a pair of dividers, you can transfer these measurements to the border.

Let's say you are launching from Swanage jetty on the south coast of England. By using your dividers on the chart you can see that your latitude is 50 36.4" north, or 50 degrees 36.4 minutes north of the equator, and your longitude is 1 57.2" west, that is 1 degree 57.2 minutes west of the Greenwich meridian. There are 60 minutes in a degree.

You enter this position into the GPS as follows: latitude 50 36.400; longitude 001 57.200. Note that the minutes must be entered to three decimal places. It is not often necessary to be this exact, but the spaces must be filled, so simply enter zeros. In some cases it is also important that the degrees longitude are entered using three figures, so insert two zeros before the figure one.

Before accepting this position, the GPS will check whether the latitude is to be entered as north or south (that is, north or south of the equator), and whether the longitude should be east or west (east or west of the Greenwich meridian). Having confirmed north and west, you can then enter the position as a waypoint.

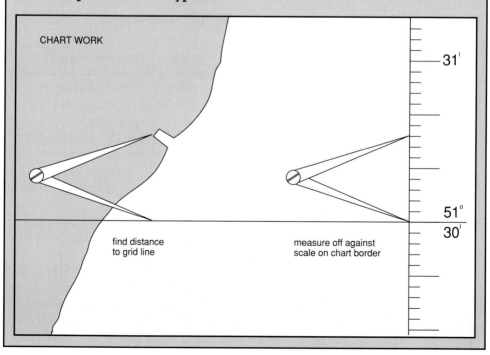

CHART WORK

31'

51°
30'

find distance
to grid line

measure off against
scale on chart border

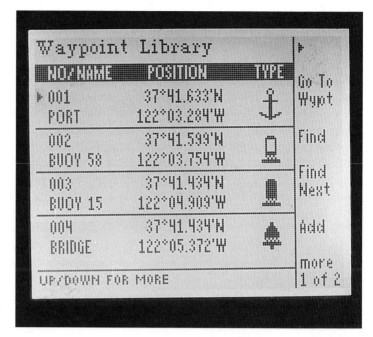

NO./NAME	POSITION	TYPE

Waypoint Library

▶ 001 PORT — 37°41.633'N 122°03.284'W

002 BUOY 58 — 37°41.599'N 122°03.754'W

003 BUOY 15 — 37°41.434'N 122°04.909'W

004 BRIDGE — 37°41.434'N 122°05.372'W

UP/DOWN FOR MORE

Go To Wypt / Find / Find Next / Add / more 1 of 2

▶ *This 'waypoint library' gives the number, description, type and lat-long position of each mark. They may be entered in order, or at random for later retrieval into a route plan.*

moored boats or even across dry land (see 'Starting error' below). You will have to ignore this misinformation and make your way to your first waypoint by conventional pilotage – so make sure it is an easily identifiable point such as a buoy at the entrance to the harbour channel.

If you are entering a series of waypoints which define your route to a favourite destination, then make a list of the positions in order. Use a waypoint sheet, as shown on page 94. Do not write on this one: use it to make photocopies (it is the only copyright-free page in the book.) If you have a word processor you can make your own waypoint sheets in any format. Fill in the name of the waypoint, the lat/long position, and the bearing and distance from the start position or previous waypoint. All this information can be derived from your chart or map. For high-speed cruising or flying the waypoint sheet is invaluable, because chartwork can be difficult or even impossible.

Entering the waypoints

Having filled in your waypoint sheet, you can enter each position into the navigator. Take special note of the east/west notation on the longitude, for unless you

| WAYPT/ROUTE/CHANGE | | | | GPS | Lat | 51°16.790′N |
| Route 0: Leg 0: Dest 0: | | | | | Lon | 0°57.572′W |

ROUTE 01:

Total Distance:	71.85	NM	°Mag
Leg	Waypoint	Range	Bearing
00	005		
01	006	22.98	291.3°
02	003	48.87	82.7°

WAYPOINT LIBRARY

No.	Name	Position	Type
001		° ′	
002		° ′	
003		50°41.713′N 1°43.647′W	
004		50°31.004′N 1°57.882′W	
005		50°27.701′N 2°26.353′W	
006		50°35.952′N 3°00.000′W	
007		50°45.000′N 1°32.000′W	
008		° ′	
009		51°11.400′N 1°27.421′E	
010		50°42.265′N 1°32.173′W	
011		° ′	
012		50°46.302′N 1°17.505′W	

▲ *The screen of this high-spec GPS shows both the waypoint library and a route plan. The waypoints can be selected from the library and placed in any order to build up a route.*

change the notation the GPS will assume it is the same as that of the previous position occupying that memory slot. In most parts of the world this works well, but if you are navigating in western Europe your route may cross the Greenwich Meridian, in which case the east/west notation of the waypoints will change.

You will probably enter the waypoints in order but this is not essential, because a separate function enables you to select waypoints at random and put them in any order you wish. The GPS will then direct you from waypoint to waypoint in this sequence. On some sets this is called a route, while on others it is called a sailplan or pilot plan. More sophisticated sets have a system of reversing the plan, enabling you to return along the same route.

STARTING OUT

Once you have entered the waypoints into the GPS you can set off from your base towards Waypoint 1 on your sailplan. As noted above, you will have to ignore the navigator display for this section of the trip, for it will direct you to the first waypoint by the shortest track

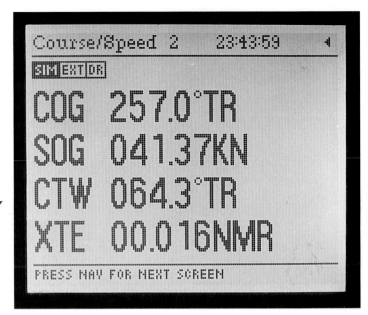

Course/Speed 2   23:43:59   ◄

SIX EXT DR

COG 257.0°TR
SOG 041.37KN
CTW 064.3°TR
XTE 00.016NMR

PRESS NAV FOR NEXT SCREEN

▶ *The course informa-tion tells you which way you are going, but the cross-track error (XTE) gives a more immedi-ate indication of your position relative to the track you marked on the chart.*

irrespective of any obstructions. But once you reach Waypoint 1 you can switch to Waypoint 2, and start using the GPS.

The set will give the distance and bearing of Waypoint 2, the course you are actually following and the speed you are making. Another display can show your ETA (estimated time of arrival) and your position in latitude and longitude. But without doubt the most valuable part of the display is the cross-track (XT) or off-track (OT) information. This is the display that indi-cates how far to one side of the imaginary track line you are. The display varies from set to set: some show arrowheads, some show dog-legs, solid bars or hori-zontal thermometer-type graphics. The better models show a 'road' heading towards the next waypoint with an indicator showing your position and orientation on the road relative to the centreline.

All of these displays indicate which way to steer and some supply a figure showing how far you are 'off track'. For example, if the tide or wind has pushed you off-course to starboard the display may put up a row of arrowheads pointing to port, indicating that you have to steer to port to correct the error. In the same situa-tion a 'road' display would show your position on the starboard side of the roadway.

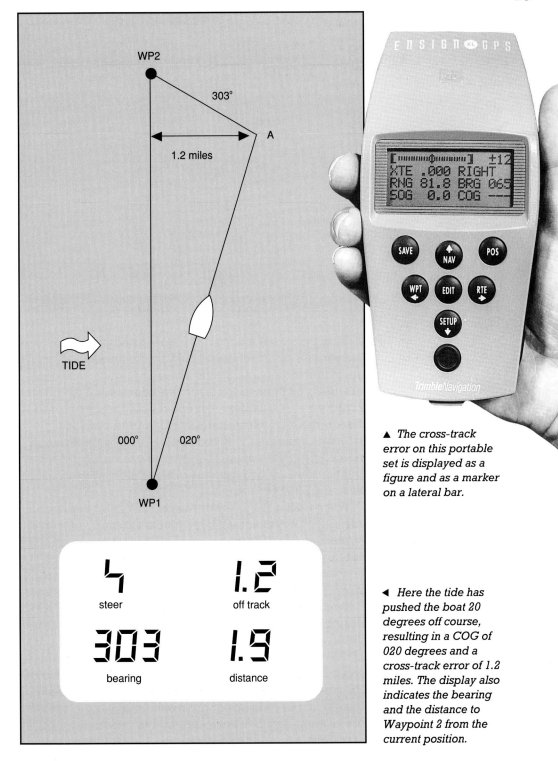

WP2

303°

A

1.2 miles

TIDE

000°   020°

WP1

[ɪɪɪɪɪɪɪɪɪɪɪɪɪφɪɪɪɪɪɪɪɪɪɪ]   +12
XTE .000 RIGHT
RNG 81.8 BRG 065
SOG   0.0 COG ---

▲ *The cross-track error on this portable set is displayed as a figure and as a marker on a lateral bar.*

◄ *Here the tide has pushed the boat 20 degrees off course, resulting in a COG of 020 degrees and a cross-track error of 1.2 miles. The display also indicates the bearing and the distance to Waypoint 2 from the current position.*

4
steer

1.2
off track

303
bearing

1.9
distance

▶ *A 'road' style steering display indicating the track to Waypoint 3. The current position relative to the track is indicated as a circle, with an arrow showing the orientation of the craft.*

This system of steering the boat or aircraft takes into account all the possible variables which could affect your course accuracy, such as tide or wind, and ensures you stick to the track you marked on the chart, avoiding all obstacles. You may think that steering to the cross-track error in this way leads to constant course alterations, but in practice you will find yourself making a slight adjustment every 30 minutes in a slow boat and every five minutes or so in a fast planing boat or aeroplane.

If the GPS is interfaced with the autopilot the course will be adjusted automatically, and the craft will run straight down the ground track. Whether this is appropriate for your particular strategy is another matter, and we will be looking at the advantages and disadvantages of steering by cross-track error in Chapter 9.

Some sets can accept information on the tide direction and speed, either by manual input or directly from other instruments such as the compass and log via the NMEA 0183 interface. This is interesting and potentially useful, but you don't actually need this information for most types of navigation. It is simpler to just steer a direct course to the next waypoint by watching the cross-track error. Another method is to note the bearing of the waypoint and check the course-over-ground;

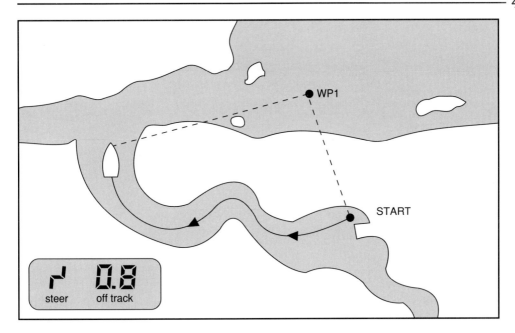

the difference between the two bearings is the compass offset required to keep you on track (see diagram on page 35). Always bear in mind that steering to this information does not involve any knowledge of the tides or winds, since the navigator's computer reduces these variables to a simple measurement of cross-track or course error which is easily correctable by the helmsman.

Starting error

Initially you may be confused by the apparently large cross-track error displayed as you head out from your start position to Waypoint 1 on your route plan. As noted above, the set starts working from waypoint zero, so it draws an imaginary line between the start position, which could be your marina berth, to the first waypoint entered. A straight line from the start to Waypoint 1 will almost certainly be radically different from your actual track as you thread your way down the winding channel into clear water, and the difference will be shown on the display as a substantial cross-track error.

On a sunny day you can simply ignore the display until you get to Waypoint 1, but if visibility is poor then you need to have accurate cross-track information to

▲ *As you motor out of harbour the navigator will try to direct you overland to the first waypoint. Here the display is indicating a 0.8-mile cross-track error and suggesting a change of course to starboard, which is not much help.*

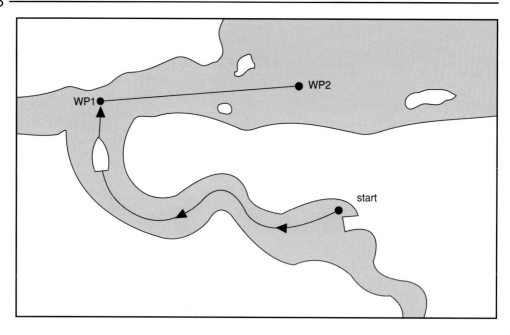

▲ *You will have to negotiate the winding channel using traditional pilotage techniques, but by entering another waypoint in the fairway you can use cross-track information to avoid the rocks on the way out to the open sea. More importantly, perhaps, you can also find your way back, in the dark.*

guide you from the end of the buoyed channel to the first waypoint (assuming this is some distance from the channel entrance). In other words, you need the set to re-draw or re-start the imaginary line from your position in clear water to Waypoint 1.

Some sets have a 'GOTO' button; just press this, enter the next waypoint number, and the set will re-draw the line direct from your position to the waypoint. At the same time your cross-track error is reduced to zero. On other sets you will have to re-start the sailplan. Some will just need you to agree SAILPLAN YES/NO while sets which have more than one sailplan will need you to enter the number of the plan you want to use.

GPS logs

Some of the more sophisticated GPS sets have another feature, a GPS log. This is a totalling log of the distance travelled by the set when it has been operating. As it updates its position every minute or so the set adds up the distances run, showing a total mileage figure on demand. A couple of units have more than one log: a non-resetting log which gives the total mileage the set has covered, plus one or two trip logs that are user-adjustable.

If you consider the way this distance-covered information is gathered you can see how valuable it is. As the GPS measures speed and therefore distance *over the ground* the memorised log measurements are remarkably accurate – much more accurate than any ship's log, which can only measure speed and distance through the water. So the distance indicated on the GPS relates directly to the distances indicated on the chart, and you can plot your position in relation to hazards without having to rely on estimates of tidal offset and leeway based on ball-park figures and guesswork. Nevertheless you should always be aware of these factors, if only to check that your GPS is giving you sensible position information.

▲ *Knowing your exact position relative to any charted hazards will give you the confidence to navigate positively, at speed.*

DEFENSIVE NAVIGATION

I always maintain a DR record to back up the electronic systems on board. Who knows what may happen? Your GPS set could break down, it could get soaked in a storm and 'drown', or the United States Government could decide to turn off the GPS system for an hour or two for repairs. Either way it is absolutely essential to record your progress throughout a voyage.

TIME	LOG	to WPT	BRG	DIS
1200	13.6	3	112	8.2
1230	18.5	3	110	3.3
1300	23.5	4	163	64.5
1330	28.5	4	162	59.4
1400	33.4	4	163	54.2
1430	38.3	4	164	49.1
1500	43.3	4	164	44.0
1530	48.4	4	163	38.9
1600	53.4	4	164	33.9
1630	58.4	4	165	29.0
1700	63.5	4	163	24.1
1730	68.6	4	163	19.3

▲ *This list of log readings and GPS information, noted at half-hour intervals, could prove a lifesaver if the electronics go down. Note that each position is noted as a bearing and distance to a waypoint for ease of plotting.*

The only way of doing this is to keep a regular record of your position, either on the chart or map or simply by taking notes. If you also record the log reading and the time of the fix, then you will have a recent position to work from if the electronics stop working altogether. On a fast-moving boat or aircraft you should note this information every 15 minutes or so but on a slower boat, a cross-country vehicle or just walking, a note every 30 minutes should be enough.

It is tempting to press the POS (position) button every time you want a fix, but if you do this you are not using the full capabilities of the navigator. In any case entering a lat/long position on a chart or map while tossing about on the waves or bouncing around in a cross-country vehicle is almost impossible.

The best method is to use the waypoint navigation function and simply note your distance and bearing to the next waypoint at periodic intervals. This position is exactly the same as your lat/long position but it is much easier to plot. For example if you are moving down a direct line to your waypoint without any major deviations to one side or the other the GPS will show whether you are on the line. If you have previously drawn the line on your chart at the passage planning stage then you already have one element of your fix; plotting your position is just a matter of using a pair of dividers to measure the distance from the waypoint, as displayed on the GPS, onto the line on the chart. This will be your current position.

To make life even simpler, mark off some distances along the line when you draw it on the chart. For example, if the distance to Waypoint X is 100 miles, mark off increments of 10 miles starting from Waypoint X. Indicate the distance of each mark from the waypoint, so they count down as you draw closer: 90, 80, 70 and so on. Obviously the increments used should be tailored to the scale of the chart you are using, and if you get it right you will find that it is easy to interpolate between the distance marks. So if the GPS indicates 35 miles to go, you are midway between the 30 and 40 mile marks: indicate your position, then add the time and the log reading.

The other essential element of defensive navigation is to use all the information you have at your disposal. If you have a Decca or Loran C set on board, fire it up and enter your passage plan. It may be less accurate than your GPS, but since it is a totally separate system it is a valuable back-up. Radar is another useful tool for the navigator. Not only can it 'see' things in poor visibility but it is an excellent distance measuring device. Maybe your next waypoint is just off a headland. The GPS is showing the DTG (distance to go) as 1.5 miles,

▼ *If you mark your chart with a cross-track 'corridor' and distances back from the next waypoint you can use the XTE and DIS displays to provide an instant position plot.*

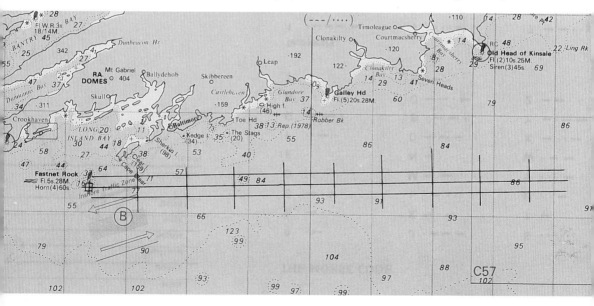

and on the radar you have a headland showing up at a range of 1.58 miles. Since the two independent machines are in agreement you can be certain of where you are.

Even if the GPS is the only piece of sophisticated electronic hardware you have on board, you can still keep tabs on its performance. Use the GPS in the same way that you use your pocket calculator: make a rough estimate, and be sure the figures on the display correspond to it. Run your DR plot as described, and make a habit of cross-checking your position by whatever means present themselves. If you cross a depth contour on the chart, check it with the sounder. If two prominent landmarks come into visual alignment as you pass, lay a straight-edge through their marked positions on the chart and see if the projected line runs

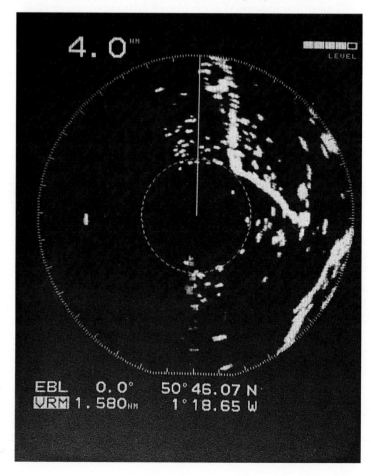

▶ The range of the headland showing on this radar screen is 1.58 nm – indicated by the dotted circle of the variable range marker, or VRM. You should use such information whenever you can to check that the GPS is working properly.

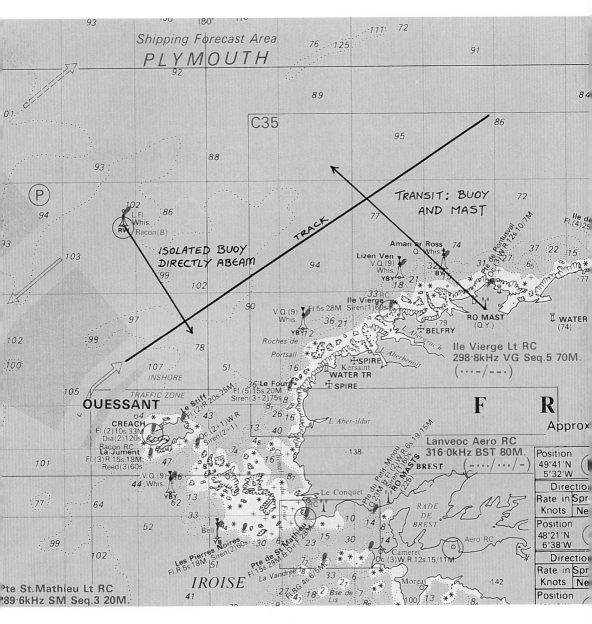

through your track line at roughly the right point. If it does, fine. Your GPS is doing its job and you know you can rely on it. But if you get a serious discrepancy you could be running into trouble. Find yet another source of information and check your position with that. You will probably find that the GPS was right in the first place, but it's good to be sure.

▲ *If you pass a land- or sea-mark, or see a useful transit (two marks visually in line) use it to check the performance of the GPS.*

Navigation on land

The advent of GPS navigation has made life much easier for hill walkers, explorers, mountaineers and cross-country drivers, for nowadays there are many pocket sets available which can give a precise position anywhere on the earth's surface within a few minutes of switching on. If the set is working in 3D (three dimensional) mode it will even give a height above sea level. When used in conjunction with a good compass a portable GPS set adds a completely new dimension to exploration off the beaten track, improving safety and confidence to unprecedented levels.

The principles of using GPS on land differ very little from those at sea or in the air: the unit is set up in the same way and gives the same information on demand. If the set is completely portable, however, then battery life becomes a major factor to be taken into account. The battery life is rarely more than two or three hours so although you must carry spare batteries and know how to change them, it is also essential to conserve power whenever possible. Luckily, for most overland purposes it is not necessary to have the GPS running continuously to supply fixes every minute or less. Indeed if you were crossing a desert on foot a fix every hour or so would be a luxury. Likewise mountaineers and hill walkers are more interested in the direction to go rather than their immediate position. This means that the GPS spends most of its time switched off, extending battery life immeasurably!

If you intend to return to base at the end of your overland trip you must establish where that base is. In the planning stage, use maps and guides that are marked in lat/long coordinates to find the exact starting position, as well as the positions of stopping places, camp sites, river crossings and pick-up points. These will be your waypoints. Note all the bearings and distances on a waypoint sheet before keying them into the GPS set, and retain the sheet as a further reference point in case the electronics should fail. During your trip you should make a note of all major changes of direction as both a lat/long position and a time. Any

significant points should be recorded in the same way
– a stream or river, a shelter hut, an oasis, a road crossing or track divide. The idea is that you can always
retrace your steps if you have to.

Keeping a course is not as easy as steering a boat or
aircraft, for nature never intended anyone to journey in
a straight line overland. Navigating by cross-track
error is impossible, for there are too many obstructions such as rivers, valleys, hills and mountains. But
this should not cause too many problems for a lone
hiker with a GPS. If you have a waypoint to head for
then a bearing taken from the set will give a direction
which, with the aid of a compass, can be translated
into a far object to aim at. Repeating this at regular
intervals ensures that you make your way steadily
towards the waypoint.

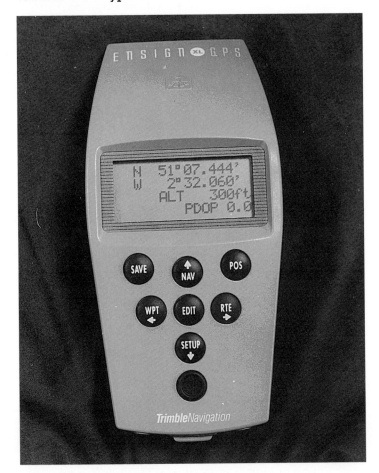

◄ This portable GPS
is showing the height
above sea level – a
figure that could be
very useful in moun-
tainous country where
altitude varies widely
over short distances.

In theory, of course, you could navigate by monitoring the COG (Course Over Ground) display, but apart from the battery drain this would incur it is hardly wise (or fun) to walk across country staring at a GPS display. You could fall down a hole.

Making notes is not easy in bad weather, for paper gets wet and pens will not write. One solution is to follow the example of underwater scuba divers, who use chinagraph pencils on 'arm slates' – small plastic boards which strap to your arm. These are ideal for wet foggy moorland hikes or steamy tropical jungles. Aircraft pilots use 'leg slates' in the same way because they have only one free hand.

If you plan on venturing out in these conditions you must make sure your GPS set is waterproof, for electronics do not like getting wet. Be warned: many of the very small hand-held sets are not waterproof at all.

If you take a fix from the set using the bearing and distance to a waypoint, then take another half an hour later, you can double the difference in the distance readings to give an average speed over the ground. Using this figure you can work out a rough time of arrival at your waypoint. You may find that, at your present rate of progress, you will not arrive until after dark. Knowing this could enable you to decide, in good time, to make camp earlier than planned at a different location.

Accurate position fixing can also be essential for setting and re-locating supply dumps on long expeditions. If you have radio contact you can coordinate air drops and rescue operations with precision. Indeed the time cannot be too far away when everyone who travels just a few miles from civilisation will automatically put a GPS into his or her coat pocket.

◀ *The advent of GPS has made extended travel in hostile wilderness regions much less risky than it once was.*

8 GPS in the air

The introduction of small, lightweight, reliable GPS electronic navigators has revolutionised the private flying market. Even the smallest microlight can now pack a GPS receiver to give sophisticated navigation information to the most basic of flying machines. Hot air balloonists are now carrying GPS sets, for not only can they see where they are being blown and at what speed, but they can radio a pick-up vehicle with a precise landing location. The pick-up vehicle – GPS equipped, of course – can enter the balloon's position as a waypoint and find the flight crew with confidence and accuracy.

Some of the most experienced pilots have completely changed their style of air navigation to exploit the benefits of GPS. For many years radio-assisted air navigation has been based on a series of homing beacons dotted around the world. A special on-board directional radio receiver is tuned in to the required beacon, and as the pilot heads towards it indicators on the set show his off-track error; when he arrives overhead the next beacon is tuned in and the process is repeated.

This system has proved reliable over many years but it does have some shortcomings. The radio transmissions are fairly low on the VHF band and are vulnerable to atmospheric and electrical interference. When using the system, you have to select a route along a series of beacons rather like stepping stones which eventually bring you to your destination airfield. This is because the range of each beacon is limited by the VHF system, which is essentially line-of-sight from the ground-based transmitters. As a rough guide, a pilot takes the square route of his height in feet and multiplies it by 1.25 – so if he is flying at 3600 feet, the square route (60) multiplied by 1.25 gives 75 miles. If the beacon antenna is on a mast and the pilot knows its height he can apply the same calculation and add the result to the 75-mile figure – so if the mast height is 200 feet above sea level the square root of this figure (44.7) multiplied by 1.25 gives 56 miles. Added to 75,

GPS has taken a lot of the guesswork out of ballooning, since it enables the back-up team to locate the balloon crew quickly and easily.

this gives a total range of 131 miles. This is not very far, so if the pilot is flying at 3600 feet throughout the trip he will not be able to select a beacon 150 miles away and fly directly towards it. Even if he does pick up a beacon on the limit of its range the signal is usually unreliable until the range shortens; if he is flying on autopilot the intermittent signals will make the aircraft dodge around the sky because of the signal variation.

All these problems are avoided by using GPS. You can now buy a GPS navigator especially designed for aviation use. It comes complete with pre-entered way-points of every beacon and airfield in your part of the world, and if you venture further afield you can load a new data file with the relevant information for the area you are flying in. Since there are no range problems you can plan your flight directly from start position to destination, provided you do not have to dodge around prohibited areas or high mountain ranges. Your flying times are shorter because you do not have to step around a series of directional beacons. You can still use the beacons, however, because all their locations are in the GPS waypoint memory. So if your local air traffic controller sends you towards a particular beacon you can call it up on the set to get immediate information on direction, distance, cross-track error and ETA.

The high operating frequencies of GPS signals mean that interference is minimal in all weathers, wherever you are. Even if your next waypoint is a long way off, the signal information your set is working on is solid and reliable, so you can always be sure of your position. If you switch on the interfaced autopilot the clean signal from the GPS enables it to steer the plane on a steady course at all times.

▼ *The high-speed navigation of light aircraft has been greatly simplified by the wide adoption of GPS.*

◄ *Low-profile aviation antennas are designed for minimum air resistance.*

One of the most common hazards encountered by small aircraft is the sudden onset of bad weather and poor visibility. If this means that the flight plan has to be aborted then an alternative airfield has to be found quickly. Using the old system the route to the field must be worked out on a chart, the correct beacons chosen and their frequencies keyed into the radio receiver. This can take some time, and inevitably mistakes can occur. But with an aviation GPS the job becomes simplicity itself. Pressing no more than two or three buttons, depending on the set, will call up the waypoint of the nearest airfield on your GPS, plus its bearing, distance and your ETA (estimated time of arrival). No fumbling with charts or beacons, more time to look out of the window and fly the plane, and much less likelihood of making mistakes.

The height information given on an aircraft's GPS is not reliable enough to use for landing and is largely ignored by most pilots. In any case the GPS gives a height above sea level, so you would have to know the height of your airfield above sea level and deduct it from the displayed figure to make it meaningful.

Installing an aviation GPS set is much like installing a marine unit, except that the antenna is smaller and well streamlined to reduce air resistance. Naturally the antenna has to be mounted outside the aircraft fuselage to give a clear 'view' of the sky and ensure good reception of the satellite transmissions.

9 Refinements

Once you have grasped the principles of navigating by using waypoints coupled with cross-track information there are many ways in which you can refine your use of the system.

TIDAL STEAMS AND CROSSWINDS

When you use traditional methods of navigation on a cross-channel voyage you may well allow yourself to be swept to one side of your track and then back again by the tidal flow in both directions. This way your vessel will cover the shortest distance through the water, saving time and – if you are motoring – fuel. It also enables you to maintain the same course to steer throughout the trip, which simplifies the navigation if you do not have an electronic system aboard. If you tried to cover the shortest distance over the *ground* by using the cross-track information to stick to the direct line drawn on a chart, you would actually cover a greater distance through the water, so it would take longer and use more fuel.

As an extreme example, consider a 60-mile crossing of the English Channel in a boat making five knots and experiencing a six-hour flood tide followed by a six-hour ebb tide. The passage time will be 12 hours, and if the tidal velocity is a steady 1.5 knots and traditional methods are used to take advantage of the tide the total distance travelled will be 60 miles. If the electronics are used to follow a direct line with tide compensation all the way, the distance travelled would be 2.5 miles longer, or 0.5 hours' extra sailing time. In a light wind the extra sailing time increases dramatically.

If the boat's speed is 10 knots and the start time is delayed to allow three hours of tide one way and three hours the other way the situation changes. By following the direct line electronically, compensating for the tide and wind all the way, the extra distance travelled will be less than 0.25 miles. In other words the journey would take 1.5 minutes longer.

So on a fast boat you may as well use the GPS to follow the direct track. On a slow boat – and this includes most small sailing boats – the traditional methods could save sailing time, but in the author's experience

▼ *If you try to stay on track in a cross-tide you will sail further.*

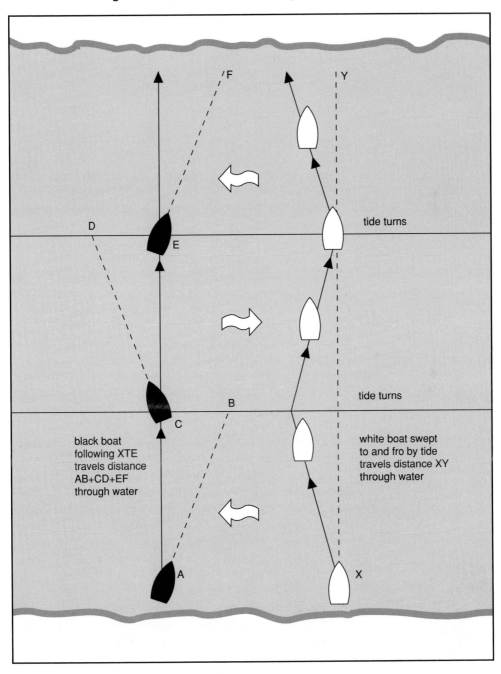

tide turns

D

E

tide turns

B

C

black boat
following XTE
travels distance
AB+CD+EF
through water

white boat swept
to and fro by tide
travels distance XY
through water

this is hardly ever the case in real life. Tidal information is, at best, not very accurate. Its flow rate can vary according to your location, its direction can vary from one hour to the next, it can vary between spring and neap flows and be affected by atmospheric pressure. Then there is the wind to be allowed for. Your leeway depends on the strength of the wind, the angle of the wind, your speed through the water and the individual characteristics of your craft. Quantifying all these factors is largely a matter of guesswork, but by using the cross-track displays and sailing down the direct line between two points all these variable factors are automatically taken into account. The electronic navigator is only interested in your position relative to the sea bed and will clearly show if you are being pushed off course in any direction from the ground track between your start position and the next waypoint.

Using the cross-track display to follow the direct line across an ebbing and flowing tide will always result in a longer passage, but on a reasonably fast boat the extra distance will not be significant enough to justify working out all the variables of tidal set and leeway. Even if you are sailing at five knots you may find that the advantages of sticking to the track outweigh the uncertainties of trying to predict the unpredictable.

BEATING TO WINDWARD

Obviously a sailing boat cannot always take a direct line to a waypoint, because if the wind is blowing from the direction of the waypoint the boat has to beat at about 45 degrees to the track to make any headway. But this does not make the GPS redundant, since if you are a long way from your destination the cross-track error can be used to indicate when you should tack.

For example, if the wind is on the nose your tacks will be roughly symmetrical about the wind direction. Select a distance to either side of the track, say five miles (checking the chart for hazards), and sail on one tack until your cross-track error is showing five miles. Then go about and sail on the other tack. The error will reduce to zero, then start to increase again as you cross your track line. When the display is showing a five-

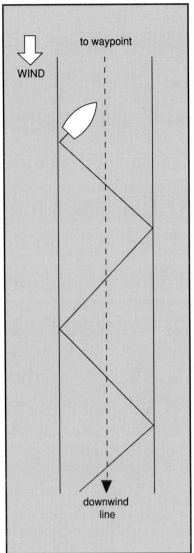

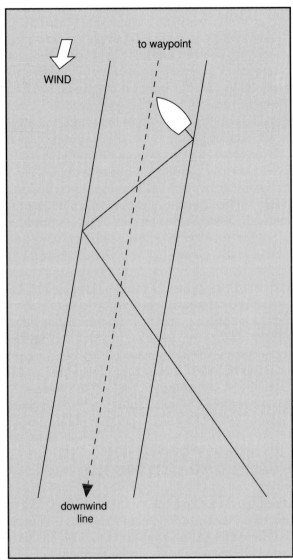

▲ *If the next waypoint is directly upwind you can use the XTE information to tack up a pre-defined 'corridor'. If the waypoint is not directly upwind, lay the corridor along the downwind line and sail into it.*

mile error on the other side go about again, and so on. If it helps, you can set up the unit to sound an alarm whenever the cross-track error reaches five miles.

If the wind is off the bow but you still have to beat, then ignore the rhumb line and draw a line on your chart directly downwind of your next waypoint. Checking that there are no hazards in the way, set up your five-mile 'corridor' to either side of this new rhumb line, and reset your navigator as you cross it. (Watch the bearing-to-waypoint and press the reset

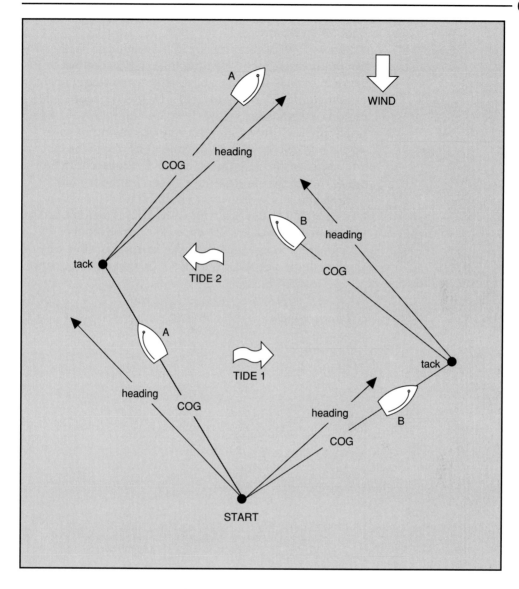

button when the display indicates the wind direction.) The set will now take the new rhumb line as the track, and you can beat down the corridor at 45 degrees to the track, tacking whenever the cross-track error reaches five miles.

GPS does not have all the answers, however. When beating, don't forget the tide: sail as much as possible with the tide on your lee bow. By tacking when the tide turns you can ensure that the tide pushes the boat to windward, and towards your destination.

▲ *By beating into the tide (left) and tacking when the tide turns you can get the current to 'lift' you towards your destination. Get it wrong (right) and you get nowhere, slowly.*

Closer to home

When you are getting closer to the waypoint, within ten miles or so, it can be difficult to judge the last few tacks to ensure that you arrive exactly on target and not downtide. The way to deal with this problem is to choose a target a sensible distance *uptide* of your destination, then draw a line directly downwind of your target and construct a 60-degree cone about the downwind line. Make sure there are no dangers within the cone, then note the bearing of each boundary line.

Now you can switch your attention from the cross-track display to the bearing-to-waypoint display. In the example the lines are drawn at 30 degrees to the downwind line, so each time the helmsman sees one of the bearings indicated on the set he can go about and

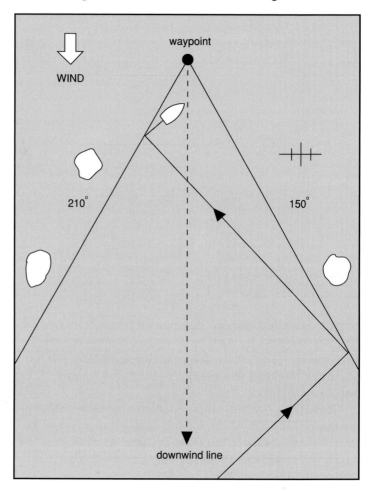

▶ *When you get near your destination waypoint, draw a 'cone' on the chart with bearing lines that clear all known dangers. If you tack every time one of the bearings shows on the 'BRG to WPT' display you will rapidly close with your target.*

start another tack. He can maintain this tack until the display shows the other bearing, then tack again, and so on.

On a long trip against headwinds you can tack between two parallel lines either side of the course until you are eight or ten miles away, depending on conditions, then use the two-bearing method to sail up a 'funnel' to the waypoint. Remember that this method takes into account all the variables such as tide, leeway, boatspeed and the numerous course changes you have to make to keep the boat sailing fast on the wind. It will not prevent you hitting a rock, however, so you must check the chart carefully for any hazards lying within your proposed corridors and cones, and modify your plans accordingly.

10 Making a trip

Let us take a closer look at an actual voyage from the Hamble River on the south coast of England to the Channel Islands off the coast of France. The plan is to make an overnight stop at Braye Harbour on Alderney, then negotiate the notorious Swinge Channel and continue through the Little Russel Channel to St Peter Port on the island of Guernsey.

PLANNING

The first step of any voyage, and sometimes one of the most interesting, is to open up the charts, maps and pilot books to decide where to go. It is at this stage that we determine our route and pick the best positions for use as waypoints. This part of the operation can be carried out at home in the comfort of your armchair, and if you have a suitable low-voltage power supply the waypoint information can be entered into the machine at the same time. It is not necessary to take the navigator antenna off the boat, however, because you will not be interested in receiving satellite signals at home (unless you want to plot your house position). The internal memory with its back-up lithium battery will store all the information you enter. Of course the 'antenna fail' alarm will buzz, closely followed by the 'Poor GPS signal' alarm, so you will have to turn these off to preserve your sanity.

Starting from Hamble Point Marina, pick out the selected waypoints on the chart. Enter the latitude and longitude coordinates of each one, plus the bearings and distances between them, on your waypoint sheet. Check each one carefully and then enter the lat/longs into the GPS.

If your set has a sailplan or pilot plan routing facility, now is the time to decide on your passage plan. The first seven waypoints will be passed in number order from 1 to 7, but when you arrive at Waypoint 7, a point off Alderney's Braye Harbour, you will turn almost 90 degrees into the harbour entrance (Waypoint 8). This

▶ Nine of the waypoints for the trip, noted on the waypoint sheet provided on page 93.

ROUTE: _HAMBLE TO ST PETER PORT_   **DATE:** _____

NO.	DESCRIPTION	LAT.	LONG.	DIS.	BRG.
1	HAMBLE POINT BUOY	50: 50: 18 N	01:18:58 W	1.0	180
	READING AT WAYPOINT:				
	LOG READING AT WAYPOINT:		TIME AT WAYPOINT:		
2	CASTLE POINT BUOY	50: 48: 68 N	01: 17: 58 W	1.6	156
	READING AT WAYPOINT:				
	LOG READING AT WAYPOINT:		TIME AT WAYPOINT:		
3	POINT OFF CALSHOT SPIT	50: 48: 33 N	01: 17: 60 W	0.4	180
	READING AT WAYPOINT:				
	LOG READING AT WAYPOINT:		TIME AT WAYPOINT:		
4	EAST LEPE BUOY	50: 46: 08 N	01: 20: 85 W	3.0	223
	READING AT WAYPOINT:				
	LOG READING AT WAYPOINT:		TIME AT WAYPOINT:		
5	N.E. SHINGLES BUOY	50: 41: 94 N	01: 33: 25 W	9.0	242
	READING AT WAYPOINT:				
	LOG READING AT WAYPOINT:		TIME AT WAYPOINT:		
6	POINT OFF THE NEEDLES	50: 39: 58 N	01: 35: 88 W	2.9	216
	READING AT WAYPOINT:				
	LOG READING AT WAYPOINT:		TIME AT WAYPOINT:		
7	POINT OFF BRAYE HARBOUR	49: 44: 25 N	02: 11: 25 W	62.2	202
	READING AT WAYPOINT:				
	LOG READING AT WAYPOINT:		TIME AT WAYPOINT:		
8	BRAYE HARBOUR ENTRANCE	49: 43: 90 N	02: 11: 30 W	0.3	187
	READING AT WAYPOINT:				
	LOG READING AT WAYPOINT:		TIME AT WAYPOINT:		
9	POINT IN THE SWINGE	49: 43: 30 N	02: 14: 28 W	2.2	252
	READING AT WAYPOINT:				
	LOG READING AT WAYPOINT:		TIME AT WAYPOINT:		

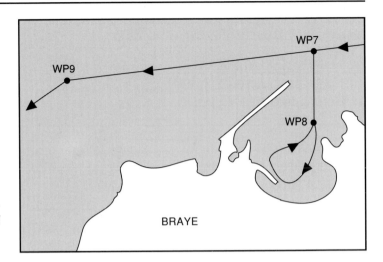

▶ *The route and way-point sequence in and out of Braye harbour on Alderney.*

is obvious, but when you leave the next day the order will not be so clear. You are at, or very near, Waypoint 8; you will then go to Waypoint 7 to get back on the route, then proceed to Waypoint 9, then 10 and so on. In short, Waypoint 7 will be entered twice in your route plan. So if you enter the waypoint sequence 1, 2, 3, 4, 5, 6, 7, 8, 7, 9, 10, 11, 12 this will allow you to make the detour into the harbour and out again the next day without resetting the machine.

READY TO GO

With the set back on board and packed with information you are now ready to leave, but before you cast off remember to switch the GPS on and let it settle down for a few minutes. Then plot your position on the local chart from the display. This ensures that the machine is working correctly and giving good information. It is always good practice to make a note of the latitude and longitude of your home berth or airstrip. Then you only have to glance at the navigator to verify the plot and you do not have to transfer it to the chart every time.

Before you leave, select the 'waypoint' or 'navigate' page on the machine, and the bearing and distance to Waypoint 1 will be shown on the display. Remember that this bearing is a straight line from your berth out to the Hamble Point Buoy, so you must ignore it – and

▶ *Chart 1 – Hamble Point to the western Solent.*

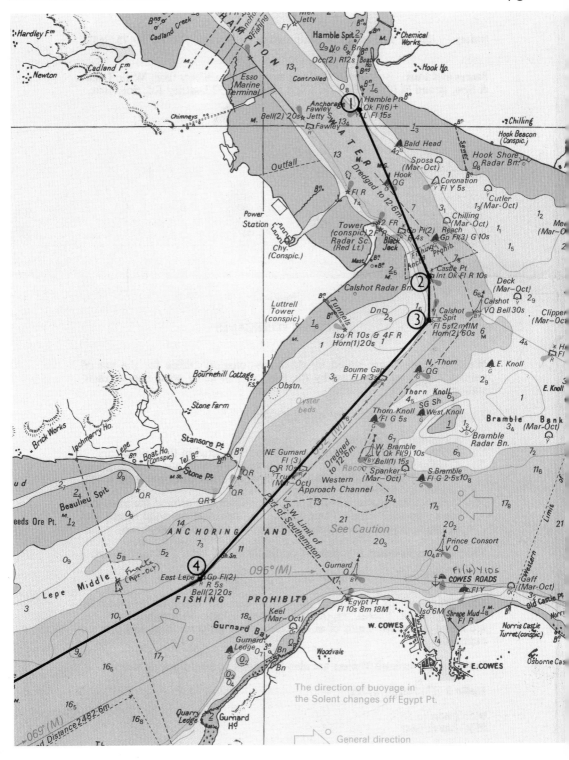

Hours before H.W.						HW	Hours after H.W.					
6	5	4	3	2	1	HW	1	2	3	4	5	6
063	097	243	260	265	267	246	194	106	079	074	074	066
0·9	0·2	0·6	1·4	1·8	1·5	1·1	0·4	0·7	1·2	1·6	1·7	1·1
0·4	0·1	0·3	0·6	0·8	0·7	0·5	0·2	0·3	0·6	0·8	0·8	0·5

Hours before H.W.						HW	Hours after H.W.					
6	5	4	3	2	1	HW	1	2	3	4	5	6
058	126	200	225	231	233	239	237	033	034	039	046	052
0·7	0·3	0·4	1·0	1·2	1·1	0·7	0·2	0·3	0·9	1·2	1·1	0·9
0·3	0·1	0·2	0·5	0·6	0·5	0·3	0·1	0·1	0·4	0·6	0·5	0·4

Hours before H.W.						HW	Hours after H.W.					
6	5	4	3	2	1	HW	1	2	3	4	5	6
047	055	120	198	205	218	219	215	285	353	019	044	044
0·7	0·3	0·1	0·2	0·6	0·8	0·8	0·6	0·2	0·1	0·4	0·8	0·7
0·4	0·2	0·1	0·1	0·3	0·5	0·5	0·3	0·1	0·2	0·3	0·5	0·4

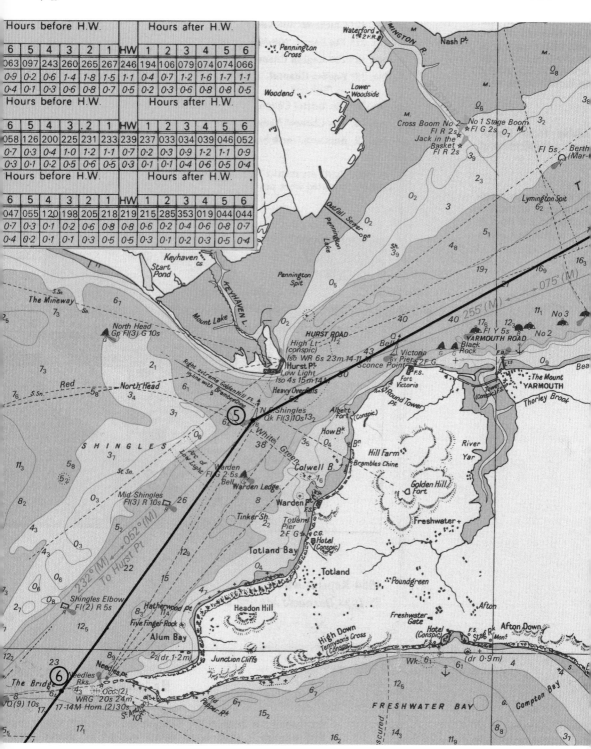

any cross-track error – as you negotiate the narrow winding channel. When you arrive at the buoy (Waypoint 1), take a note of the lat/long reading on the set and note it down in the correct box on the waypoint sheet for future use.

If you have entered a route or sailplan then the set should automatically switch to the display for Waypoint 2, but if your set does not have a route or sailplan facility enter Waypoint 2 as a 'GOTO' location. In this example we left at high water, so by now the tide is starting to ebb down Southampton Water. The bearing of Waypoint 2 is shown as 161 degrees, but if you steer this course for a few minutes a cross-track error will begin to grow and the arrows or graphics will suggest you alter course to starboard to compensate for the ebbing tide pushing you off to port.

You can alter course by a few degrees and watch the display to achieve an optimum course by trial and error, but a more scientific method is to bring up the COG (course-over-ground) display before you make any course alteration. This may show a COG of 156 degrees: a difference from the bearing of six degrees. This means you are being pushed off course by six degrees, so you should add six degrees to your course of 161 degrees to give an optimum 'course to steer' of 167 degrees. On arrival at Waypoint 3, the point off Calshot Spit, you follow the same procedure to the next waypoint, and so on.

After leaving Waypoint 4 the course takes you along the Solent. If you have set a steady cruising speed of 10 knots then you can note the SOG (speed-over-ground) reading to see the actual speed you are making over the ground. On a spring tide or with a following wind the SOG reading could be 12.5 knots. This means you are gaining 2.5 knots over your cruising speed as the tide and wind help you along. On this leg the tide may be easing you off course a little to starboard but the cross-track display will soon show this up, indicating a slight correction to port to keep you on track for the next waypoint. Remember to note the lat/long readings each time you arrive at a waypoint. Then add the ship's log reading and the time. This will give you a good fix to work from if the electronics stop working.

◀ *Chart 2 – The western Solent and the Needles Channel.*

THE LONG HAUL

Once around the point off the Needles Lighthouse at the Western end of the Isle of Wight you will be heading out into the English Channel, on course for the Island of Alderney 63 miles away. The tide will be flowing down-channel, and as in the Solent a cross-track error will start to show on the display. As before, the simple solution is to note the bearing to the way-point and check it against your COG (course-over-ground). The bearing should be 206 degrees and your COG could be 211 degrees, a difference of five degrees. You should subtract this from the bearing to the waypoint because the tide is flowing from port to starboard, so 206 degrees – the bearing to waypoint – minus five degrees gives a new course to steer of 201 degrees.

The tide flowing in the English Channel is never constant in velocity or direction, so further slight course adjustments will have to be made *en route*. This usually amounts to a slight course change every half hour or so, allowing you to maintain steady progress while fully compensating for tide, leeway and varying boatspeeds.

It is imperative that a regular position fix is plotted on the chart or noted down, together with the time and ship's log reading. Look at the waypoint display and note the bearing and distance from the next waypoint. This is easier to remember than a lat/long position and absolutely identical since both figures are calculated by the internal computer from the same information source.

It is good seamanship to keep a lookout at all times, both for other large ships and smaller yachts and motor cruisers making the same course (or its reciprocal) as you. These people could be employing electronic navigators and using the same waypoints as you – in which case they are running up or down precisely the same track. One of the negative aspects of the accuracy of modern navigation equipment is the increased risk of electronically-aided collisions!

If you are sailing and the wind is uncooperative, forcing you to beat to windward, then select a suitable distance each side of the downwind line and tack to it.

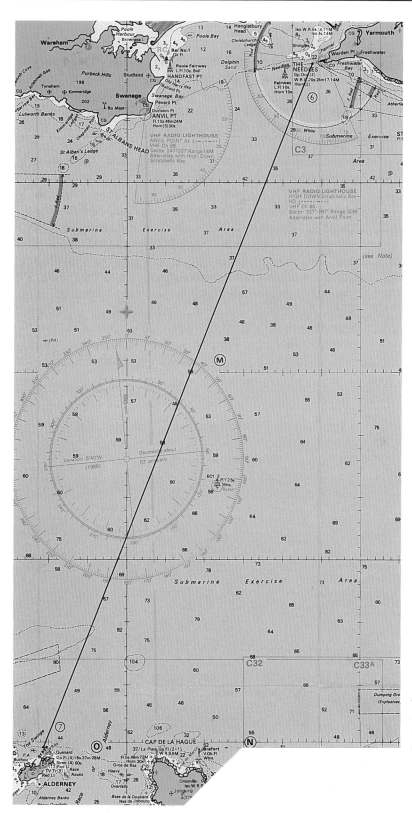

◀ Chart 3 – The long haul from the Needles to Alderney.

For example, if you decide to tack five miles either side of the line, reset the GPS as you cross the line and sail close-hauled until the display shows a five mile cross-track error. Then go about and tack back the other way. The error will reduce to zero then start to increase in the other direction. When you reach five miles again go about and repeat the exercise.

This method can be used very effectively until you are within eight miles or so of Waypoint 7. At this point you have to arrange things so you arrive slightly uptide of the waypoint, so draw two bearing lines on the chart from a point just uptide of Waypoint 7 – one line at 251 degrees and the other at 193 degrees. Call up the waypoint display on the GPS and look at the BRG (bearing to waypoint) figure. Continue sailing until the bearing shows 193 degrees, then go about. Keep on the same tack until the bearing shows 251 degrees and go about again. Sail back to bearing 193 degrees and so on. In effect you have created a 'funnel' from Waypoint 7 which you are tacking into on

▼ *Chart 4 – Alderney, Braye Harbour and the Swinge.*

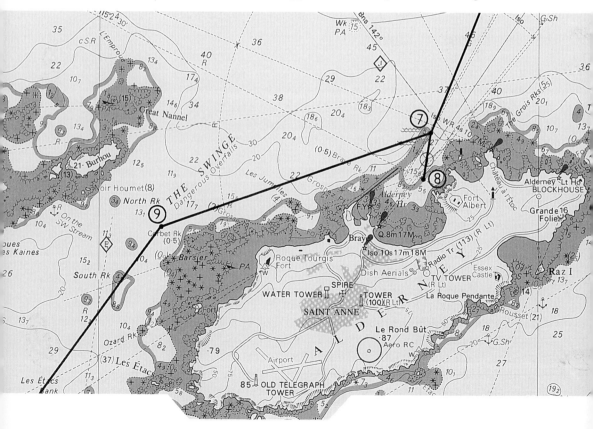

shorter and shorter legs until you reach the waypoint. Remember that this information from the set takes into account all tidal, leeway and boatspeed differences on any heading.

ARRIVAL AT ALDERNEY

At Waypoint 7 you turn to port and head for Waypoint 8, the entrance to Braye Harbour on Alderney. Be sure to note, on the waypoint sheet, the position reading shown on your set when you enter the harbour. The next time you are here the harbour may be hidden in thick fog, and in such conditions you will want to be able to return to this spot with confidence.

From Waypoint 8 you enter the harbour and pick up a visitor's mooring. The navigator can now be turned off. The internal battery will keep the memory active, so all your waypoints, date and time information will be preserved until you switch it back on.

ALDERNEY TO GUERNSEY

Next day, turn the machine on just before departure and allow time for the set to acquire the day's satellites and give a steady position reading. Check the position to see if it is accurate, then cast off. Motor along the line of visitor's mooring buoys and then turn out of the harbour entrance heading for Waypoint 7: the point off Braye Harbour.

If you look at the navigator at this stage it will be showing a large cross-track error, indicating that you should turn to port – but if you follow its advice you will hit the harbour wall! The error is showing because the navigator is working on a line from your overnight mooring buoy directly to Waypoint 7, the point outside the harbour. So ignore this cross-track error and reset the machine by re-starting the route from Waypoint 8.

The next waypoint after Waypoint 7 is Waypoint 9. On this leg you must keep a strict watch on the cross-track error because the Swinge Channel is not very wide and is flanked by dangerous rocks on either side. On reaching Waypoint 9, the one in the Swinge, alter

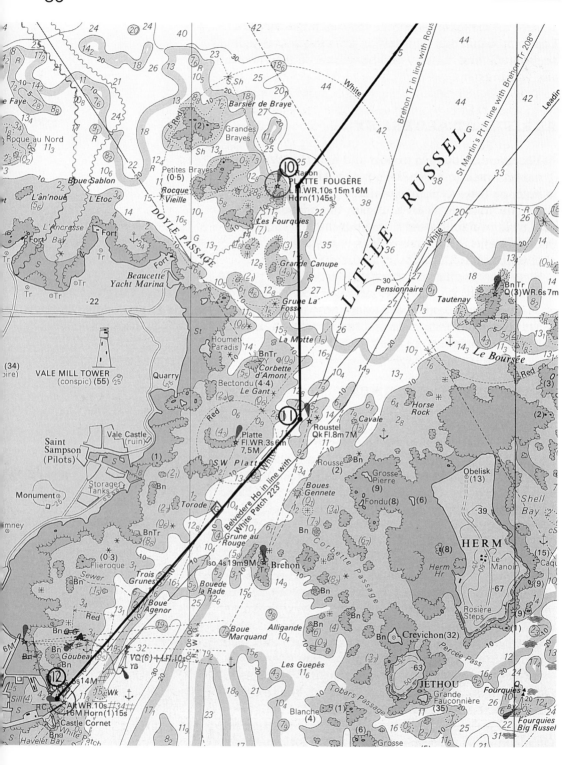

course for Waypoint 10 off the Platte Fougère lighthouse on Guernsey. On this leg it is essential to keep
to the track line as the infamous Pierre au Vriac rock
lies to starboard of your course and is unmarked!

The tides are variable in direction here depending
on your start time so you must keep a careful eye on
the GPS display and make any small course corrections it suggests. Use these opportunities to activate
other functions on the set such as COG (course over
ground), and call up the ETA (estimated time of
arrival) to plan your arrival time to coincide with the
sill gate being open. Of course you must continue to
plot your position on the chart at regular intervals; if
your power fails in these waters you will soon be in
serious trouble if you do not know exactly where you
are.

Waypoint 10 is off the Platte Fougère lighthouse
which you leave to starboard. The next leg brings you
down to Roustel Tower, Waypoint 11, which is left to
port. Then comes the final approach to Waypoint 12, St
Peter Port harbour entrance. After the relief and the
thrill of completing the passage do not forget to take a
final position reading when you are midway between
the harbour walls. On a dark foggy night you will be
very grateful you took this reading, since it will enable
you to find your way back in the worst visibility.

◄ *Chart 5 – The Little
Russel Channel,
Guernsey and St Peter
Port.*

11 GPS errors

To protect the military interest the GPS system for civilian users has been degraded by the addition of SA, or Selective Availability. The specifications state that the accuracy of SA working should be to within 100 metres but in practice, over many thousands of miles, the author has found that the general accuracy is around 65 metres. This may seem poor compared to the potential accuracy of the system, but for most practical purposes it is a remarkable improvement on the accuracy of Decca or Loran C navigators. Loran C can manage 200 metres at best, and although Decca can work down to 50 metres both these low-frequency navigation systems suffer from electrical interference, weather conditions and land distortions of the signals which dramatically reduce their accuracy and are not necessarily predictable.

SA can affect the computation of the SMG (speed made good) or GS (ground speed), as well as the CMG (course made good) or GT (ground track). These readings can fluctuate wildly on earlier GPS sets, but later models have introduced a better smoothing system to iron out the fluttering SA signal so the readings are much steadier.

Chart datums
The fundamental error that 90 per cent of GPS users experience is chart datum error, which can give inaccuracies of 200 metres or more. The GPS system is based on a chart datum derived from the World Geodetic System 1984 (WGS 84); by contrast many charts are based on datums derived from local systems of projection, so you *must* apply corrections if you transfer your GPS position to such a chart. The British Admiralty charts are based on 1936 OSBG Datum, most of the European coastal charts are based on European Datum ED50, and there are a host of other datums in use throughout the world.

On each chart the datum is normally marked next to the title: 'For satellite derived positions the following correction can be applied'. It then gives a difference to be added to the latitude and the longitude. This can be laborious, but there is an easier way.

All GPS sets have a selection of datums programmed into them, and choosing the right one enables the set to make the correction for your chart automatically. Look at the datum on your chart, then select the same one from the list given on the GPS. Make a note of the datum the GPS is using and stick it somewhere prominent, so when you change charts you can check that the datums agree. If you are careful about datums GPS navigation is unbeatable in terms of consistent accuracy – anywhere, and at any time.

On the subject of datums, there are some traps to avoid in connection with electronic chart plotters. A chart plotter is a computer that can display chart information taken from a magnetic cartridge or CD-ROM disc. The problem is that each cartridge or disc stores a number of different charts, usually of different datums, so when you switch screens from one chart to the next your datum may change without your knowledge and your plotting accuracy can be up to 200 metres adrift. So if you are contemplating buying a chart plotter ask the salesman to look at the cartridges or CD-ROM discs supplied. Look closely to see if they are marked with a datum. If not, the charts are a mixed bag and will not be consistently accurate. Try another plotter manufacturer to see if their data is marked. If it is, your GPS can be programmed to agree with your plotter, with consequent improvements in accuracy.

Chart errors

Another barrier to accurate navigation is the basic accuracy of the original chart survey. For example, some charts of the Caribbean Windward Islands are based on a survey made in the 19th century, and you may find that your GPS is giving you a position half a mile inland on the local chart.

This is where it helps to take lat/long positions and note them down on the waypoint sheet. This way you can always return to those particular waypoints by calling them up on the GPS and ignoring the suspect chart. Eventually you will build up your own library of accurate positions, enabling you to interpret the chart with more confidence.

12 Advanced functions

Many of the GPS navigators on the market are packed with 'goodies' that will never be used, but some of the more useful ones are waypoint management systems and sunrise/sunset times.

Waypoint management

Waypoint systems allow you to transfer and copy waypoint information between different sections of the waypoint memory banks. Some sets have an additional waypoint bank, enabling you to download a waypoint instantly by pressing one button. So if you wanted to record a favourite fishing spot or swimming hole you can simply push the SAVE button (or whatever your set has) and the position is dumped into a memory slot. On some sets the waypoint saved in this way is allocated the next available waypoint number, while on others there is a separate 'dump' section capable of retaining ten positions. Later on you can call up the waypoint management pages and transfer these waypoints from the 'dump' memory to the conventional waypoint memory.

▶ *At the press of a key you can save your current position and either copy it to the library as a waypoint for future use or – in the case of a man overboard – instruct the machine to guide you straight back to it.*

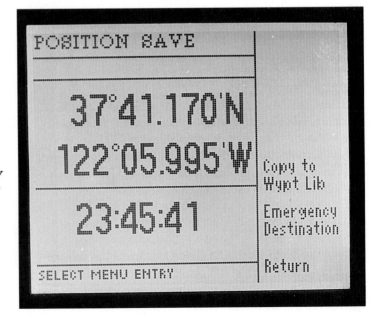

SATELLITE INFORMATION				
SV Locked	02	16	17	26
SNR	10	25	10	23
Elevation	44°	61°	22°	51°
Azimuth	131°	198°	302°	288°
SV Used	02	16	17	2

◄ *The status display on the GPS, showing which satellites are providing information, their signal-to-noise ratio (SNR), elevation, azimuth and, by implication, their dependability.*

Another way of entering a waypoint is to give the set a range and bearing from your present spot. If you want to go to another place that is five miles away on a bearing of 326 degrees then you just enter these two figures. Within a second or two the set's computer works out the lat/long position and enters it into the memory slot.

Sunset and sunrise

Sunset and sunrise times can be obtained from some receivers. If the relevant page is called up it gives these two times in local time. If you want to know the sunset or sunrise time at a distant waypoint, however, you can enter the waypoint number and the set will work out the times at your destination.

Satellite exclusion

There is always a possibility that a satellite may become faulty and will not respond to the control station in the USA. Sometimes satellites are taken out of service for a while, or have their orbits changed. Warning notices of such developments are broadcast on the International Navtex system, and in the unlikely event of a rogue satellite giving false information some of the top-of-the-range sets have a satellite exclusion facility. If you enter the number of the appropriate satellite your set will ignore its transmissions, so the suspect information is excluded from any position-fixing calculations. When the satellite is healthy again you can take out your exclusion parameters and the system will work in the normal way.

13... The theory of the system

It is not necessary to read this section! Knowing how your set works does not make you a better navigator or operator. Nevertheless you may wish to know more about the system you are trusting with your life.

The GPS, or Global Positioning System to give it its full name, is a satellite-based navigation system that provides accurate time, velocity and position information. Each satellite transmits a number of accurately timed signals as well as a navigation message; this includes information that is used to determine the time these signals were transmitted, where the satellite was at that time, and any satellite clock corrections. The receiver notes the arrival time of each signal and then calculates the range of each satellite based on the known speed of light. Given the range, the computer linked to the receiver can calculate the unit's position if the elevation is known – as it is when you are at sea.

The transmitted signals consist of two high-rate, bi-phase shifted key codes. The 'P code' signals are intended for military use and the 'C/A code' signals are for civilian consumption. As the frequencies are very high the signals are resistant to most forms of electrical interference including other radio signals, electronic equipment and the weather.

Dilution of precision

In two-dimensional GPS navigation each satellite effectively generates a circular line of position on the earth's surface. All points on the circle are the same distance from the satellite concerned, and the circle is moving constantly. When two satellites are in view two circles overlap, giving two crossing points. Since the receiver knows it is somewhere on both circles, it could be in one of two positions. If a third satellite – and circular position line – is brought into the equation the possible positions are narrowed down to one; adding a fourth provides a measure of height.

The accuracy of any radio navigation system depends on the geometry of the situation. Since the GPS satellites are constantly moving the calculated crossing angles are always changing, and the effects of this are summarised in a single number called the Horizontal Dilution of Precision (HDOP).

The accuracy obtainable from a particular set of satellites is equal to the error in the range measurements multiplied by the HDOP. Most receivers have a pre-set limit which excludes satellites that give an excessive HDOP value. Some sets allow the user to set the limits but in all cases the lower the figures the better the accuracy. The figures can be checked by calling up the 'status' display on the unit which will show the HDOP of each satellite in view.

Selective Availability

The United States Department of Defence has adopted a policy that will limit the performance and accuracy of GPS signals available to civilian users. A cryptographic technique 'dithers' the clock speeds in a random manner, and this causes errors in timing. To the end-user these errors are quoted as up to 100 metres. This degrading system is known as Selective Availability (SA).

Some receivers have full access to the 'Y Code' transmissions for correcting the 'dithered' satellite clock and ephemeris data. These Precise Positioning

▼ *As with any fix, poor geometry can increase the potential error. If the satellites are well spaced (left), their arcs of position – which are subject to slight range errors – cross to give a fairly tight fix. If the satellites are close together (right), the effect of the range errors is magnified. Luckily most modern GPS sets are equipped to prevent this type of problem arising.*

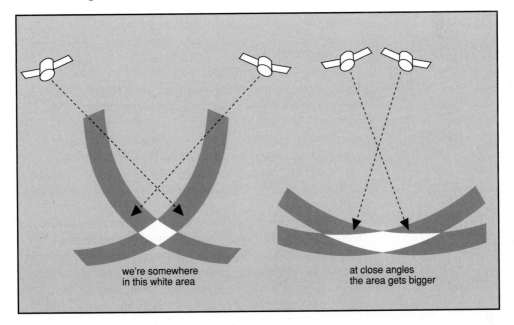

we're somewhere in this white area

at close angles the area gets bigger

Service (PPS) receivers are restricted to special operators and will not be available on the open market.

In practice the average fix error associated with SA is plus or minus 65 metres. The occasional large fix error – sometimes up to 200 metres – rarely lasts longer that a few seconds, so at a second glance the receiver will be giving a different set of figures. But which is right? If you have been monitoring the trend, as you should, the answer should be obvious.

The speed-made-good or speed-over-the-ground figures can also be affected by SA. Speeds can jump up and down by five per cent while course-made-good bearings can flicker a degree or so either side. When SA was first brought into operation many GPS sets suffered badly in these two respects. The second-generation units now on the market incorporate improved averaging software and this has smoothed out many of the fluctuating display problems.

The life of SA is uncertain. Some experts say it will be used for two or three years; others say longer. Its future may be affected by the Russian Glonas satellite system, which works on the same principles as GPS. Some Glonas satellites are already in orbit but the system is not yet completed. If the signals from Glonas are not degraded, so the accuracy is better than GPS, the United States Government may have to think again about SA.

Differential GPS

The accuracy of GPS can be improved by a technique call 'differential GPS'. This works by putting a GPS receiver and transmitter unit in a permanent, known position. The unit acts like a static reference point, transmitting error-correction data to any suitably-equipped receivers in that locality. The accuracy achieved by this technique can be within four metres and some survey sets can work to accuracies of within one metre!

Basically the differential reference set is mounted at a very exact surveyed point. It receives the transmissions from the current satellites and works out the calculations 'backwards' – that is to say it knows exactly here it is and it knows where the satellites are, so it can work out the distance between itself and each satellite.

The distances are divided by the speed of light and a time figure is arrived at. The differential set checks this 'apparent time' against the calculated time to give corrections that can be applied to the 'dithered' time information broadcast by the satellites. The corrected time can then be used by suitably-equipped sets to compute accurate positions.

In short, instead of using time signals to calculate a position, differential GPS uses a known position to calculate a time.

RECEIVER TYPES

There are various types of GPS receiver. Each can give accurate information, but the more sophisticated designs can give more data, slightly better fixes and faster updates.

Continuous receivers

These can monitor four or more satellites simultaneously and their data processing speed is lightning fast. They are especially suited to high-velocity situations such as aircraft or fast-moving vehicles.

Single channel receivers

These are the small, hand-held units in which power consumption from the limited battery capacity is a primary consideration. Power drain is minimised by using a single channel which switches from one satellite to the next. Because they have to do a 'round robin' and calculate each set of data their update time is relatively slow – maybe only once or twice a minute. Since they are working on less data for less time they are also less accurate than their big brothers.

Fast multiplexing receivers

These sets are similar to the single-channel receivers, but the switching time from one satellite to the other is much faster. While it is 'listening' to one satellite the internal computer is processing the data from the previous one, so the overall result is faster update times and increased accuracy as more fixes are being computed per minute.

14 Applications

The applications for GPS are countless. The most obvious one is marine navigation: there are some 20,000 merchant ships around the world and many more private boats, and they all need an accurate, reliable navigation system.

Accurate navigation is obviously important from a safety point of view because otherwise dense traffic in coastal areas and shallow waters can lead to shipwrecks and loss of life. Apart from this, however, the requirements differ from one marine user to another. Cargo vessels, oil tankers, bulk carriers and passenger vessels have one thing in common: they need to transport goods or people from one place to another in all weather conditions in the minimum time and at the cheapest price. A dependable navigation system eliminates one area of risk and makes the job that much

▼ *Differential GPS offers surveyors an easy-to-use mapping tool of unprecendented accuracy.*

easier; it also enables the ships to run the shortest distance between two points using the minimum amount of fuel.

By comparison, a fishing boat has different requirements. The fisherman needs to return to exactly the same position to retrieve gear time after time, and fishermen need to record the position of new fishing grounds with as much precision as possible. Only electronic navigation systems can provide this precision, and only GPS is capable of providing it worldwide.

Oil and gas exploration

Oil and gas exploration at sea is not new, but the greater accuracies offered by GPS are enabling seismic surveys to be carried out with great precision over wide areas. Drilling rigs using differential GPS can drill for samples and send back the core pieces to laboratories on land; if the results look promising then the rig can go back and put the drill bit down the *same hole* to explore further.

Land applications

On land the system can be used for surveying, for rescue services, and for a variety of purposes in cars, trucks and trains. In the USA experiments are currently being run using GPS receivers on trains coupled to radio transmitters. The base stations receive the signals which tell them where the train is and how fast it is moving. GPS is already starting to appear in cars, linked to map displays projected onto the windscreen.

Aviation

Differential GPS is starting to become the primary navigation system for civil aircraft. In addition smaller sets are used in helicopters for sea rescues, offshore transportation and flying into isolated areas for military or humanitarian missions.

Surveying

Using the very expensive P-code receivers and differential GPS, surveyors can work to accuracies of within a few centimetres. The system is the most accurate available for surveying and building tall skyscrapers.

15 Waypoint sheet

This waypoint sheet has been designed as a blank template for photocopying. There is space for nine waypoints on each sheet, but by taking several copies you can record the details of as many waypoints as you like. The sheets can be filed for future reference.

Route and date
Fill these in if you are using the sheet to record the waypoints of a particular voyage.

Waypoint number
For a voyage, the number of each waypoint should correspond to the route or sailplan. This is the order in which they are entered into the navigator. So Waypoint 1 is the first to be reached on the trip, Waypoint 2 the second, and so on.

If you use the sheets as a filing system you may prefer to number the waypoints by a different system, and alter the numbers to suit your route or sailplan when you transfer them to the navigator.

Description
Enter the name of the waypoint if it has one; for example 'St Peter Port Harbour Entrance', or 'Point off Needles'. Otherwise identify the position as best you can and add any distinguishing marks that may help you recognise the waypoint, such as 'Castle Point Buoy, red can'.

Lat and long
The top two coordinates should represent the position of the waypoint as indicated on the chart.

Distance
Fill in the distance of each waypoint from the last, as measured on the chart.

Bearing
Under this heading, fill in the bearing of each waypoint from the last.

ROUTE: _____ **DATE:** _____

NO.	DESCRIPTION	LAT.	LONG.	DIS.	BRG.

___

READING AT WAYPOINT: _____
LOG READING AT WAYPOINT: _____ TIME AT WAYPOINT: _____

___

READING AT WAYPOINT: _____
LOG READING AT WAYPOINT: _____ TIME AT WAYPOINT: _____

___

READING AT WAYPOINT: _____
LOG READING AT WAYPOINT: _____ TIME AT WAYPOINT: _____

___

READING AT WAYPOINT: _____
LOG READING AT WAYPOINT: _____ TIME AT WAYPOINT: _____

___

READING AT WAYPOINT: _____
LOG READING AT WAYPOINT: _____ TIME AT WAYPOINT: _____

___

READING AT WAYPOINT: _____
LOG READING AT WAYPOINT: _____ TIME AT WAYPOINT: _____

___

READING AT WAYPOINT: _____
LOG READING AT WAYPOINT: _____ TIME AT WAYPOINT: _____

___

READING AT WAYPOINT: _____
LOG READING AT WAYPOINT: _____ TIME AT WAYPOINT: _____

___

READING AT WAYPOINT: _____
LOG READING AT WAYPOINT: _____ TIME AT WAYPOINT: _____

___

Reading at waypoint

The lower two coordinates are filled in as you reach each identifiable waypoint (such as a buoy) taking the figures from the GPS display. If there is a slight system or chart error these coordinates could be slightly different those you entered from the chart. If you return to this waypoint then use this second set of lat/long figures since they will give greater accuracy and cancel out any smaller errors; as a result you will return to exactly the same spot every time.

Glossary

C/A code The standard coarse acquisition code information transmitted by GPS satellites, and available to all users.

CD-ROM An audio-type CD loaded with digital data, such as the chart information employed by chart plotters.

Chart datum The system of mapping used to define positions on a chart. The datum used by the GPS must correspond to the chart datum if position fixes are to be related accurately to other charted objects.

Chart plotter An electronic plotter that shows your position on a representation of a chart or map.

Course made good (CMG) The actual course followed by the craft, rather than its compass heading.

Course over ground (COG) *see* Course made good.

Cross track error (XTE) Your position relative to the track line between two waypoints, displayed as the distance you have strayed to one side of the track.

Deviation Compass error induced by onboard magnetic influences.

Dead reckoning A system of finding a rough position by calculating forward from the last good fix.

Differential GPS A highly-accurate refinement of the GPS system based on corrections broadcast by special ground stations.

Great circle A radius from the centre of the earth which constitutes the shortest distance between two points on the globe.

HDOP The Horizontal Dilution Of Precision, or margin of error, associated with any GPS fix.

Heading The compass course and apparent direction of travel.

Interface The electronic code that enables two devices, such as a GPS and an autopilot, to pass information back and forth.

Leeway The amount a craft drifts under the influence of the wind.

Log reading at waypoint

Read the log when you reach the waypoint and enter
the figure here. This will help you keep a DR (dead
reckoning) track of your position.

Time at waypoint

Note the time when you pass the waypoint. If the GPS
stops working, the time and the log reading will
enable you to work out a current dead-reckoning position from the last waypoint.

P-code The precise code that is available only to military users.

Rhumb line A direct line between two points, as marked on a normal
chart.

Sailplan A list of waypoints in route order.

Selective Availability (SA) The deliberate degrading of the GPS signal
by the US government to protect military sites.

Speed made good (SMG) The actual speed achieved by the craft over
the ground or sea bed, rather than its speed through the air or water.

Speed over ground (SOG) *see* Speed made good.

Status display A display on the GPS showing the positions, signal
strengths and reliability of the signals broadcast by the satellites in view.

Starting error The spurious cross-track error indicated by the set on the
way to Waypoint 1 on the route plan.

Track The proposed route between two waypoints, and the line that the
GPS will assume you want to stick to.

Track plotter An electronic plotter that shows your track and any waypoints on an effectively blank screen.

Universal Time Coordinate (UTC) The standard time used by GPS systems (for all practical purposes Greenwich Mean Time, or GMT)

Variation The difference between magnetic north and true north – which
varies according to your position on the globe, and from year to year.

Velocity made good (VMG) The actual speed you are making towards
your destination, even if you are moving in a different direction, as when
beating to windward in a yacht.

Waypoint Any chosen position entered into the receiver as a destination.
The GPS will guide the craft in a straight line until it reaches the waypoint.

Waypoint dump The facility to save the current position as a waypoint
and 'dump' it into the waypoint memory.

Also published by Fernhurst Books